The Mirror In The Brook

Mark Hamilton

ISBN 978-1-63525-319-1 (Paperback)
ISBN 978-1-63525-320-7 (Digital)

Christian Faith Publishing, Inc.
832 Park Avenue
Meadville, PA 16335
www.christianfaithpublishing.com

Printed in the United States of America

Contents

The Cry of Love 13
The Eyes of Jesus 14
Land of the Free and Home of the Brave 15
An Unshakable Foundation for Love 16
Born in Sin..17
Emotional Eruption 18
Timeless Pieces 19
God's Gift 20
The Winds of Hell..21
Deception 22
A Cryogenic State of Mind....................................23
My Love...24
Please Remember Me 25
Hook and Crook...26
Mental Heartache..27
A River of Peace 28
In The Last Days...29
Not Analytical..30
An Empty World...31
My Precious Mother..32
It Must Be a Dream...33
I Must Move On 34
A Life Worth Living...35
A Moment in Time 36
Hate..37
Sometimes I Disappear.......................................38
The Dark Comer...39
My Reality...40

Nothing Else Matters 41
I'm Not in Love...42
A World Ripped Apart 43
Looking for Answers 44
Fear of The Unknown 45
The Circle of Life 46
I'm Not That Kind of God 47
Why Do You Cry?..48
Breathe...49
The Broken Road 50
Love Has No Limits 51
Book Ends..52
In the Garden of Time..53
My Spiritual Death..54
The Untold Story 55
When I Kneel and Pray..56
Obsession...57
Locked Away...58
Jail...59
It Belongs to Me..60
My Love is Gone..61
Goodbye My Love..62
The Press 63
Heart of Love 64
The Lost World of the Grave 65
Emotional Killers 66
The Heart of a Viper 67
Dialogue of the Dead 68
World Beyond the Wall...69
The Miles of Pain 70
Are You Sure You Love Me?...71
Just Another Chance 72
Love 73
No More Pain 74
My Reflection 75
The Rose for a Woman..76

Earth's Hell..77
A Feeling Such as This..78
Cry of the Innocent..79
A Pleasant Heart..80
Spiritual Freedom..81
Another Day 82
Perfect Pieces of a Puzzle 83
Fear and Faith 84
You Made Me Strong 85
From Hell to My Tranquil Mind 86
When My Heart Cries for God 87
Can We Work It Out? 88
The Highest Praise...89
I'm Going Home..90
Yesterday's Dead and Gone......................................91
Hold onto Your Faith..92
Cry of the Angel..93
The Forgotten Past 94
He Will Always Be With You 95
Healing Waters...96
She Knows 97
Free Again 98
Unrealistic Expectations 99
The Power of the Pen...100
Life of the Undying..101
The conquered Soul..102
A Future of My Own 103
His Solemn Grace 104
Given to The Wind 105
Safe, Secure, and Warm...106
I Yearn for Your Forgiveness 107
Who Knows?...108
The Key to Your Heart 109
You're A Child of God..110
The Playing Field..111
A Pillar of Fire 112

Shadows in the Evening..113
A Hungry Soul..114
The Master of the Clouds...115
In The Reaper's Hand..116
My Spirit Cries..117
An Empty World 118
Spirit of the Laboring Crush...119
The Calmness of the Earth 120
Easter 121
The Breath of Life 122
The Forgotten Past 123
The Shepherd's Voice...124
Beyond the Sun...125
He left the Throne..126
A Divine Purpose 127
I'm Just Me 128
The Passionate Writer...129
Torn 130
Depression 131
When Love Hurts..132
A Distant Land..133
Watching the Sun..134
God's Sweet Peace..135
A Brighter Day Ahead 136
The Other Side of Heaven 137
Judge Me Not!...138
I'm Your Ego 139
Torture Because of my Sin..140
The Plea 141
I Sat Alone 142
The Flame 143
The Scroll..144
I Love Your Tender Touch 145
A Touch from Your Nail-Scarred Hand
    What Did I Ever Do to Deserve Thee? 146
When Dreams Come True..147

The Trinity 148
"Daily Points to Ponder" 149
The Spirit Within 150
In Time of War..151
A War-Torn Soldier 152
The Star Light Moon...153
Take This Memory from Me, Lord 154
Buried in the Past 155
Close to the Grave...156
The Song of Years 157
Grandmother 158
The Mind of a Jealous Heart...................................159
Strangled by Love 160
The Mirror in the Brook Written by Mark Hamilton 161
Book Cover "The Breadth of Life"...........................162
The Captain 163
The Field of Roses 164
A Lost Loved One 165
The Weight...166
Frailty of Emotion...167
From the Cross to Prison and Back "Broken Dreams,
    the Mended Soul" 168
If You Bury Me, I Shall Live 169
Close to the Sun...170
Pieces of a Bleeding Heart 171
Yesterday Is Dead and Gone 172
Can You Hear Me? 173
I Can't Save the World...174
Soft Moments 175
The Haven of Death...176
The Trials of Life 177
The Gift 178
New Beginnings 179
Stolen..180
I Believe 181
Rumors 182

Death of a Servant..183
Held by Faith 184
His Abundant Love 185
If I Could Leave the Earth.....................................186
Prayers of Stone...187
Forgiveness..188
Faith..189
The Eye of the Storm..190
The Love of God 191
My Loving Father...192
We Found Love 193
The Prince of Heaven 194
The Poet That I am...195
His Unconditional Love 196
When My Heart Cries for God 197
My Serenity is Love..198
The Cross I Have to Bare......................................199
Treasure in a Peril 200
If I could Go to Heaven 201
Until the Very End 202
The Land of Entanglement....................................203
Jesus, You're the Answer..204
God's Gift (A Special One's for Me) 205
The Rapture Has Come...206
The Dream 207
Birds..208
The King 209
The Comforter 210
The Presence of God...211
911...212
Hurt...213
The End of the Ages 214
The End of Me..215
He Hears Your Cry..216
The Cry of the Wind...217
Sober Freedom 218

The Chosen One 219
Through the Fire 220
Beneath the Willow..221
This Heart..222
What is a Friend..223
Suicide 224
Loss of a Tranquil Mind 225
He Changed His Mind...226
Safe in His Arms 227
Somewhere in the Clouds..228
Dialogue of Resentment..229
The Spiritual Wind...230
Dry Bones..231
When Mountains Fall 232
I'm Locked in My World..233
A Crooked Mile 234
In The Heart of Man 235
Earthly Treasures 236
The Price for Obedience..237
The Angel of Death 238
The Second Coming..239
My Golden Glove...240
The Child that I am..241
The Turtle..242
When Tears Begin to Fall (He Hears Your Cry) 243
Satan's Enemy...244
On a Lonely Road..245
The Throne of Grace 246
The Day He Set Me Free 247
A Divine Purpose 248
The Eastern Corner of My Window 249
I'm Just Me 250
Tired Eyes 251
Shattered Heart...252
He Knows You're Alone...253
If I Could Wave a Magic Wand 254

Possible Fate 255
Rose Petals 256
Can You Still Believe in Me?.......................................257
Still Searching 258
Until We Meet Again 259
Our Magical Love 260
The Battleground 261
Old Centralia Road...262
Eternity...263
The Last Supper 264
The Eye of the Savior..265
Lonely Heart 266
The First Day 267
The Unbreakable Truth...268
When Grown Men Cry 269
In My Dreams...270
A Field of Loneliness 271
Parental Warriors..272
Loneliness 273
The night Becomes 274
Push 275
Under The Stairs 276
The Inmate Way 277
The Rock...278
A Broken Heart That's Crying 279
The Transition of Change 280
I Wish It was Just a Dream 281
A Sinner's Prayer...282
Unknown Fear 283
A Walk Through Pain...284
The Ice Cap..285
My Lonely Existence 286
Tears..287
The Burden 288
Peace 289
Life Ever So Changing...290

Flight to Freedom...291
A Mothers Love..292
The Gift That He Gave...293
Is It Really All About Me and You?....................................294
Broken 295
Words 296
Codependent Me 297
A Mother's Day 298
The Master of the Clouds 299
His Undying Love 300
Crippled by a Plague 301
My Loving Father 302
The Abandoned Child...303
The Rapture 304
It's Bigger Than I...305
When Jesus Died to Live 306
The Mysteries of God..307

The Cry of Love

From a broken heart, Jesus gave his life. His flesh was torn; he bled deeply that night. Alone on a cross with Mary at his feet, where was the love when he died for you and me? In the heart of man, what happened that day but the cry of love?

The Eyes of Jesus

By prayer and supplication God answers with strength, given to all who seek his face. His love is abundant by the tears he has for you. When your times are troubled, He always sees you through. The glow of his spirit will shine all around and his eyes will pierce the slightest sound. He knows your heart and He always sees your pain, but to him it's only just a little rain.

Land of the Free and Home of the Brave

Across the sea, across the land, our soldiers take a stand; power and might within their hand. With all of us in mind, they fight for our freedom. By the war, wrong or right, they allow us to sleep at night. They left their families to bring peace to our hearts and no matter how hard they could never depart. Willing to die, they continued to fight. They saw an end but there, was no light.

An Unshakable Foundation for Love

An unshakable foundation for love is only given from our Lord above. We hold each other through troubled times and we always have love on our minds. The bond we share grows stronger each day and even in silence we know just what to say. Two hearts joined as one; and we lay in the sand under the sun. On moonlit nights we stroll along the beach, hand in hand by the sea and the gentle breeze.

Born in Sin

Oftentimes I fail the Lord. What does He think of me? I know I'm forgiven for my sins because He died upon a tree. He gave His life on a cross and shed His precious blood. He did this for all sinners lost. It was Jesus and His love. I try to do the best I can and fail Him many times but my Lord He understands; that's why He gave His life. He is my Father, I'm His child. I know it's in my heart. He knows that we were born in sin and He knew this from the start.

Emotional Eruption

Sometimes your life has no meaning. Your insides grind at you. There's no rhyme or reason; just an awful feeling. Changes take place all the time. The merry-go-round roller coasters everywhere in your mind. Your thoughts fly like pieces in a storm. The aftermath of devastation; then, you're awakened to a road of silence. You ask yourself where to begin and pour your ashes where you've been.

Timeless Pieces

Broken parts of my life have been scattered abroad. I've searched for answers and found one in the midst of the deep while plagued by displaced notions of triumph to conquer and overcome simple adversity.

God's Gift

You may say you're not much. What is there to give? I see no talent in myself. For what purpose do I live? I always struggle from day to day, trying to find my way. I know a place just for me given by His grace. I oft complain to myself, there must be more to life but all I find is obstacles. It seems there's always strife. In His words I know it's true, I have gifts and talents, too. If I look within my mind, I'd be surprised of the things I'd find. For God gave us all these gifts for all of us to see, and these gifts you may have but a special one's for me.

The Winds of Hell

It's not a breeze which blows through the trees. A magnificent gale, the winds of hell. It's the life of a violent storm; a tornado from the cold to the clash of the warm. A position of fate, a curse, and a spell. The winds of hell.

Deception

Liars from the pits of hell; ignoring your feelings, not caring about the real you, not being true. Living a life with a fake image. Being despiteful in the matter of their corruptible ways. They watch you fall with laughter one moment at a time, and then you crumble to sand if you allow them to defeat you.

A Cryogenic State of Mind

Deepening the heart of my existence, I'm trying to find some peace from the bitter cold smell of the past. I'm wondering how I found myself locked in a domain of the unforgiven, chasing memories that will never be again. There's no satisfaction where I lay. An exclusion from one society to another, and now having a cryogenic state of mind.

My Love

You've graced my life with your charm. I love you. I want you in my arms, your poise and your tender care, hopes, and dreams. Soon you'll be here. An Angel of light you are to me; with your love I feel free. The trust of God, the depth of my heart, A pleasure of desire, the love of you and a quiet fire, and we shall never depart.

Please Remember Me

As you look across the Sea, the oceans are filled with tears. A long life of love this had to be. What kept us together for years? When I look across the sun a memory comes to mind of dancing with the wind. We were so in love but it ended inside. Think of all the good times, the fragrance and not the grief. The way we met and fell in love; please, remember me.

Hook and Crook

Hook and Crook, that's my name. I'm evil where I am. Be rest assured I'll catch you, I know right where I stand. I'm not at peace with myself. I know you like a book. When we talk, I'll read your face and grab you by the look. I'll prey upon your weakness and try you every time. When I'm gone you won't know you've lost every dime. I'm so subtle. "Yes, it's me!" I've taken you by surprise! You can't believe I was there but I saw it in your eyes.

Mental Heartache

My heart cries out when I'm in pain. My mind won't let me be. Sometimes I feel like life's all in vain. Please, let my Spirit free! I try to do the best I can each and every day; for my only salvation is God's plan, so I continue to pray.

A River of Peace

I'm a deep person, as you can see. I search for inner strength. My mind will drift across the sea. At times I feel it sink into the depths of my Soul. Once the prisoner is released and all the answers I won't know; but, I'll find that river of peace.

In The Last Days

We have spent our time doing as we please, and our disobedience spawned a great disease. The cries of each Country just can't understand the anger of God against the sinner's hand. His power and might, we're beginning to see because of His son who hung on a tree. This is not the beginning; or, is it the end? The wrath of God has fallen again. The Pharaoh in the Bible left a deafened heart for those to see a world ripped apart. It's been a joke to the scoffers each day but the end of time is on its way. Look at the news, what do you see? The quake of the Master who died for you and me. As the tsunami rolls and the waves get high, where is your heart when God begins to cry?

Not Analytical

Real experiences have blown through our past. We've burned bridges; had relationships that didn't last. We started on a quest for love; forgot all about our Father above. Our attitude led to our demise and then ourselves. We began to despise. No light was seen for many a mile, so we gripped our drugs just for a while. There came a time when we were beaten, stayed up for days, and hadn't eaten. We pounded our brains for what we thought was good. Drugs drove us insane. We did what we could. We cried out to God many of times but the great grim reaper plagued our minds. Chaos and emptiness filled our head so many times, we wish we were dead. The turning point came when we gave up this game. We realized we were consumed by our own rules; every drug we took made us such fools. The books will teach us how to live but the hell we've been through shows us how to give. We stumble and fall and dust off our feet. We get up again and we share and we meet. Life begins to happen, good and bad, and our fellows will hold us when we are sad. When our heart breaks, and often it does, going to a meeting is definitely a must. Our days get better as time goes by, and the love of the fellowship will wipe the tears from our eyes.

An Empty World

When we have run a vicious race and feel our heart has been misplaced, we'll grab and hold on to anything because we've lost the future's dream. Our will is strong but even still our days are long as we climb the hill. If we could find the wayward path, the Spirit of God would cease our wrath. Although our heart knows the way, the sinner's prayer has gone astray.

My Precious Mother

I want, you to know you mean so much to me. You're my precious mother and my everything. Your love is strong and you are wise, and you dry my tears when I cry. Although I am so far away, not a day passes that you don't pray. Your grace and understanding has always brought me through, mama, you gave birth to me and always shows me what to do. You did your best with what you had, I'm so sorry! At times, I made you sad. You have always brightened up my day when you told me the things you would say.

It Must Be a Dream

I can't believe that I'm in here, apart from all the world. I didn't plan my life this way; I wish I'd read His Word. I should've listened to my peers when they talked to me. They were wise in what they said. It's something I couldn't see. Evil lurks in different ways, it traps and brings you down. You don't know until you're snared until you're chained and bound. There's a map. It's the book to guide and direct our path. If we don't take time to look, we'll reap a deadly wrath. It's too late! Now the time has come. It's only jail for me. I didn't think that I'd be here! I wish it was just a dream.

I Must Move On

As time goes on I can't look back. I'll pierce my mind with pain. The venom of the lost world still remains the same. Mistakes I've made, things I've done, will shadow my spirit again. Darkness will crowd my heart but I must move on and pursue my dreams

A Life Worth Living

My life begun as a young lad, confused, angered, and scared. For some of you who have been sad, I know because I've been there. I didn't think that I'd ever find even one grateful day. It seemed I was always pushed aside when other children played but my mother taught me well. She made me go to church. Yes, it's true that I rebelled. I snarled and I joked. I didn't like to hear of God. I felt He hated me but He knew the steps I'd trod, and He set my Spirit free. I started believing in His Son; that Jesus died on the Cross. I found a life worth living now. I'm no longer lost.

A Moment in Time

You came to me like the golden sun. You brightened up my day. We wanted to go to the beach but didn't get to play. But a special moment came about when you began to cry. I was there to hold you then and be by your side. You see, I want you more to myself for all but selfish things. Your inner beauty is a gem and you mean much more to me. When times are hard and you are down, I'll hold your little hand because you are a special one, and baby, I understand. So when you cry I'll wipe the tears from your pretty eyes because we have a special bond made by the bluest skies. I know it hurts when you're in pain and really hard to take, but God above knows your name. He made no mistake. You see, you're just as special to Him as you are to me. When times are hard and life is tough, only let it be.

Hate

Disgusting smells of bitter hell drawn to the evil of fate laid in wells of putrid lands at death's door, you'll find the gate. The smoke of your tongue lashes till numb as your eyes turn red The pleasure with a smile when you hold your gun and watch the calm of the dead

Sometimes I Disappear

At times my mind is empty—no thought, no place, just space. My bones are relaxed. No expression on my face. My eyes are focused, a permanent fixation. No rhyme or reason, I'm in another dimension. Alone, I sit frozen in time. Only for a season, I failed to mention my heart is quiet inside. Although people are near, sometimes I disappear. I don't fear, just hide.

The Dark Comer

In my mind there is a place from time that's left behind. A feeling that I'm all alone, my hurt is deep inside. The loss of friends from time before when love was so alive. For in my comer my heart is sore, I feel I want to die. In this comer there's just no end to the pain that I feel. Hope is lost except for memories which no one can steal. It's such a small crevasse, this space inside a small tiny place where all my scrambled thoughts will hide from God's solemn grace. If I don't come out, I'll fall away; be devoured in a while. If I stay, I'll contemplate as my mind travels the miles. To change this course, I must confess, this is my choice to lay my lonely heart to rest. I'll listen to God's voice. The dark comer is no place for anyone to be. It's eerie and it's deep. It is a deep dungeon with no return where only demons sleep.

My Reality

Today is where I truly am. I'm stuck here in this place. I'm learning lessons as time goes by. Today this is my space. I look for answers, they don't come. Why? It's just so hard. At times, I feel I want to run, but then I see the stars. God has a plan for everything. If I won't sit and whine, and will take each day as it comes, my destiny I'll find.

Nothing Else Matters

We live our life one day at a time. We try to make small plans and designs. No matter what the future holds, we set our minds on continuous goals with all the plush and clatter. Heaven only matters.

I'm Not in Love

I'm not in love but much in like. There's thoughts of you in my dreams at night. You spring with laughter and a funny grin. I'm glad, so glad! You are my friend. A spark; it's something in me that only I can feel. Your pretty eyes gaze at me, there's more to be revealed. I feel alive when I'm with you. I have not felt this in a while, but truly you're a gift from God and I love your pretty smile. You're my heart's desire, from your head to your toes. I even like your little neck and your little nose. If I can have you close to me, I'll never let you down. I'll always be a friend to you even when you frown. Yes, it's true I want you now. That's something I can't hide; but life's too short, let's take a chance on what we feel inside. This is not a ploy or plot to try and sway your mind. We're just friends and that's okay for we have plenty of time.

A World Ripped Apart

War again, haven't they learned? War is a monster of grief, the shadow of a thief. One strike can burn a soul into a blaze of deceit when warriors meet. The grunge of the earth and the broken heart of God.

Looking for Answers

Where are you this day in my mind? For some reason, the sum is hard to find. I plot and I ponder each day as it comes, and though I often wonder if maybe I will run. I'll look for the answer one day at time until I have peace. And serenity is mine.

Although my thoughts are scrambled and misplaced somewhere, God has the answer and he really does care. When I think and wonder which direction to go, I'll look to the sky and the answers I'll know.

Fear of The Unknown

My mind says, "Don't cry, it's only thunder." But my fear makes me wonder what will come next. Will it strike north, south, east, or west? My Faith must be surmounted with prayer. I must believe I'll be alright, that God's somewhere. I try to not think of this pain but it's in my brain. The tunnel is dark with only a little light. As long as I breathe, I'll fight. Twenty-four is all I have so I can't be sad. This happened for a reason, there's a meaning in the clouds. I must grab a prayer from my heart and give it to God. For brief moments I'll break inside, but God sustains me. The power of this evil is more than I can bear. This unknown fear, it rips, and it tears.

The Circle of Life

I stepped aboard a train, had Jesus in my heart. Let Him out when it stopped, for my heart was ripped apart. The days began to darken as the train rolled down the track. I waved goodbye to Jesus for His closeness I did lack. Through all the hills and valleys, my heart began to burn.

I forgot the Master as the train began to turn. I told the conductor I left my friend behind. Satan said, "That's okay; cause now your Soul is mine." I reached for the brake as I thought of the King's love. My heart began to quake. From the window I saw a dove. I told the conductor, "I refuse to ride this train." Then I saw Jesus, we were together once again.

I'm Not That Kind of God

You, blame me for all the troubles that you have, and when your heart is hurting it makes me very sad. To know that you're my child, and I love you so much and you make me smile, and I'm there when times are rough. You will never know the love I have for you. I am your loving Father. When you know not what to do, I am always with you. When it seems that I don't care, you must know I'm your God and I am everywhere. To lift and uphold you when you see there is no way. I will speak from my Spirit and guide you through the day.

Why Do You Cry?

Why do you cry when Jesus is always nearby? He will wipe the tears from your eyes. He knows your life. He knows your strife. He is your Father and He is always by your side. Through the valley He will walk with you. He really loves you. His heart is pure and true.

Breathe

Passion and love fills the air; not a worry, not a care. Full of joy and harmony everywhere. The finest hope, the magic moment, the true light, the butterfly in the sky. Just relax with every breath and breathe. The flower in bloom, the stars and the moon, the son, the cross, and the throne, and heaven, we call our home. Over oceans, land, and seas, one day we will leave. But today, we'll just breathe.

The Broken Road

Cracks and crevasses, miles of pain, miles of strain, the future seems far, far away. We don't have the answers today. Time will come and time will pass, but the broken road seems to last and last. To last forever with uncertain dimensions and mountains of fear, but the new road seems oh so near. We walk this road with all thoughts in our mind, and pray for the new life time after time.

Love Has No Limits

As high as the mountains, as deep as the sea, love has no limits for you and me. As bright as the moon, as shiny as the stars light-years away, it isn't really too far for us to hold each other's hands. Love has no limits like millions of particles in the sand. Love has no limits, as deep as the ocean's depths. Love has no limits when two hearts rest. Time is only time, and miles only miles. Love has no distance to a beautiful smile.

Book Ends

Enslaved by anger as a child, a feeling of emptiness and lost without grace, broken and shamed by the look on this child's face. Space and time have gone away but silently remain. To live a life without a map and no direction to this or that. Devalued by others, the lie and the cheat and the laughter from the devil's mouth as you begin to sink. Cries of help are released from your heart. God! Where were you when I was torn apart? Abuse is a game, for those who like to play, but it's never fun when a child has to stay. You hope and pray but you can't get away. A child with no say but it doesn't matter anyway. Some move on and have good families, indeed. And others, as adults, continue to bleed. There is no excuse for mental cuts. To destroy the mind one moment at a time, do you love it that much? The little ones that you see, just look in their eyes, are they free? This is the story. It's all about the sin. Is this how the book is supposed to end?

In the Garden of Time

I walked through the garden on a cold damp morn. My eyes began to rain. The mist of my tears fell to the ground, and my heart was grieved with pain. The garden seemed forever, like there was just no end. I forced myself through the weather, then lay in the garden of sin. An Angel came before me as I stayed fast asleep. My Father in Heaven adored me but He began to weep. He said to the Angel, "Bring my child. Bring my child to me." He washed me with the blood of Jesus the day He set me free.

My Spiritual Death

My self-will took me there because at the time, I didn't care. To gratify my flesh was my defeat. My Spirit had begun to die. From my head to my feet, I knew it was wrong to walk in the flame. But in my mind there was something to gain. The sin that I caused finally caught up with me so I live with the prisoner in my head. My Soul cries out for some inner peace. Only darkness is found because my Spirit is seized. If l could change the past, I'd rewrite the script. I would've followed a road on the narrow trip. You reap what you sow. It's said in the word. Because of my sin I'm bound to this Earth. As the days go by, I remember my sin and can't sleep at night. I hope God's still my friend until I have peace. My Soul won't rest. If my temple isn't God's, I'll feel my spiritual death. As I toss and turn, my Soul wants to burn. My Spirit grieves for peace. I await by the hour to face my demise from all the decay. My Spirit continues to cry so I pray. My only recourse is to reach for the Lord and hope that He is there. I continue to die and as I lie, I'm in the valley of full despair I knew the way but I chose to play with evil, and the rest I continue to cry because my Soul won't lie as I die this Spiritual Death.

The Untold Story

Life doesn't matter but Heaven really does. There truly is a throne of grace, and we came from dust. The Bible tells a story of the things yet to come. Jesus and His glory will shine like the sun. When He descends from Heaven high up above, He will gather His children. For God is the Father of love. Excuses are something that goes like this, and if we don't see Him, eternity we've missed.

When I Kneel and Pray

An angel stands by me when I kneel and pray, as the Holy Spirit guides me and tells me what to say. At times, my heart is hurting. Events rush through my past, but I know one thing for certain, this pain can't ever last. I gave my heart to Jesus when I was very young, but I have a problem restraining pen and tongue. So when my heart is weary throughout a given day, silent words are spoken as I kneel and pray. When you get so angry and you don't know what to do, just give your hurt to Jesus and He will see you through.

Obsession

Fifteen phone calls, no rest for I am weary. Thinking about this makes me dreary. Making love happen, that just never will. I torture myself with negative zeal. My life isn't over, just a bad love. I've got to stop this craziness and reach high above. It was sick anyway, this relationship of mine. I'll be true to myself for the very first time!

Locked Away

A place where time is no more, only concrete blocks and steel doors. Ghosts walk the halls; they have their eyes on you. Dead silence at night the inmate sleeps, and lost freedom has separated them from your love. You stand alone unless you find one who cares. Relief doesn't come from God because payment is still due. What is sin worth to you? Isn't it good you're not there?

Jail

Jail is a box, a concrete tomb, a feeling, of doom, a private hell! A bitter smell. Jail locked away, bound by thoughts, total distraught, day by day. So where can you pray? Jail, you're a foreigner, a mourner, a griever of a sort, to the guards you report. Jail is a mind trip where evil lurks and abound, Men put you down. You're in a constant fight, no sleep at night. Jail is a grave. You're a slave and your family is away. Jail is full of hate. Relief can't wait. Is this your fate?

It Belongs to Me

I couldn't blame you because I wasn't free. By my own devices, I just couldn't see. I set my course and it was very cold. But who was to blame? I corrupted my own soul. No one could tell me. I was sure to fall. It didn't matter, I knew it all. I really can say, I didn't care. Now I see why they put me there.

My Love is Gone

Yesterday we were lovers but today we're only friends. Your lips were like clay, we didn't touch, and something came between us. Your eyes stared into space. No closure here, just a sad look on your face. With only mystery, wicked wonder, what has taken place? Where did you go? Because I was here all the time.

Goodbye My Love

I, remember your tears, the day, they took, me away. I, remember, your fear, I saw, it in your eyes, I saw, it in your face, then we both started, to cry, so very sad to say. I was bound, by the law, I held, you in handcuffs, I loved, you so much. I felt, all along, you wouldn't stay, when I said, goodbye to you, that very day. Forever, I'll go away, and again, I say, "good bye my love." I'm sorry, I went away.

The Press

Thank you all for what you've done. Because of you, a miracle has come. Thanks for caring with all your hard work; for the words you printed, the time and effort. More recognition you deserve, with all the hundreds and hundreds of words.

Heart of Love

When I think of you, it's like a rose in bloom. A Spring, a flower, a heart in tune, and a time for me and you. A soft touch, a tender kiss, eyes with a mist, a tearful rain, and streams of joy. Candles of love, cards, and gifts; it doesn't get any better than this. When evening comes, we draw the shades together and then, we kneel and pray while holding each other until the very next day. Fast asleep, and the closeness, we feel, and this Heart of Love can only be real.

The Lost World of the Grave

It's over now and never to know, just the experience yet blow by blow. No more pain just Spiritual Bliss. No more rain or eyes of the midst. No more frowns, just smiles of joy. No more downs, it's like a new toy. This child I feel is alive and free. You're inside; you're the real me. I once was lost in so much despair. Today, sun shines because it cares. God is up there, He watches. He looks at me close, sees a heart that is free. He takes in a breath, a sigh of relief, to know that His child now has inner peace.

Emotional Killers

Chaos seems to wrap their heart, a yearn for the sick to depart. They'll devour your mind like chips of broken glass and they're not happy without bringing up the past. They're very sick; will pass it on to you and move in subtle ways for your Soul to subdue. Go away from the dead as far as you can. For if they drain you they were never a friend. A mind of decay is all that they know, and with their sick power they're not a friend just a foe.

The Heart of a Viper

Evil lurks with the notion of venomous pain from the bite of the snake. It's fangs drip with poison bent on destroying your mind. Who unleashed this creature inside? The serpent is subtle, it tells lies. This species lies in wait to devour its prey. This element is of the human kind, seasoned with bitterness from being hurt. The look of the cat's eye is hard and unchanging.

Dialogue of the Dead

It's jails, institutions, and death. The life that I see, the stories never change. The rippers inside of me, and they are driving me insane. Our minds are willed by the passion we feel when we are higher than high. For we destroy every part of our being while we try to reach the sky. Realities are a myth, it goes something like this: when we push our brains to get a fix, we are tricks and we play the dead game. It started before we needed much more to find some peace within. We trashed our minds as we died inside, hoping to find a friend with a joint in hand, cocaine was the plan, meth would fill our head. The drug on the side with the dealer we'd ride, and the dialogue of the dead.

World Beyond the Wall

Inside the fences is where I exist, I know there' s life outside of this. People are working and the children are at play, but for me it's just another day. Towers surround the ground inside, if you wanted to run there's no place to hide. I was stricken because of my sin, so I must remain serene within.

The Miles of Pain

It seems so insane, the miles of pain. It seems like life will never be the same. You search for truth and it doesn't make sense. Life is so intense. Then the sun glimmers before your eyes and a new day is coming again. Do you see it in the sky? Is God nearby? Is He still your friend?

Are You Sure You Love Me?

You say you love me with unspoken words. You know I want to be heard. Your eyes tell a story. You cling, too. Do they tell me the truth? Is it really you? Does peace hide behind your heart? Are you sure you love me? Did you know this from the start? Did you mean it when you said that we would never depart? And do you share your emotional scars? So near but yet so far. Do you hold on to the past and has this memory been removed at last? Are you okay today? Honey, how do you feel? Again I ask you, is your love truly real?

Just Another Chance

If I could do life all over again, I know where I'd begin. I'd have more love for others, my day would never end. I'd spend more time with Jesus, read His word and pray. Trust in Him to guide me each and every day. I'd store my treasures in Heaven so my ways wouldn't eat them away.

$\mathcal{L}ove$

It's pleasant to the touch. it's what we desire. We want it so much, that burning fire. Love surrounds our heart and engulfs every part. This love that we're seeing cradled by the arms of a babe. This love we finally made. The gentleness of the free was made for you and me.

No More Pain

Spiritual growth is all I see and a new life is given to me. A positive reflection from the midst before. No thought of regret and I won't slam the door. I must remember from where I came, to continue to grow and a new life to gain. More will come as time goes on; a mirror of disease. It's not the old me because now I'm free.

My Reflection

I look in the mirror a low countenance I see. Is it someone else or the real me? I'm tired of fighting the way of the drug. Bankrupt from the emotional twist, I want to feel the Spirit. It's something I miss.

The Rose for a Woman

This token that I give to you is from a lonely heart. I know of all I put you through. I've been sorry from the start. I wish I'd tried harder then, but I was always late. I should've been much more a friend and I know I've sealed my fate. Honey, please forgive me for what I've said and done. I'll try to make it up to you if you won't bolt and run. The mistakes I've made have cursed your heart. I can't undo the past. If I'm just given another chance, I'll change day by day. I know I truly broke your heart. I promise you I'll stay. With this rose I give to you. Please, hold it in your hand, because you know when I'm with you I'm your only man. I know your heart is shattered. I know it's ripped and torn. Please, take this token of my love for you. I will adorn.

Earth's Hell

Crime descended to streets of blood, money is the motive. Fine cars, fast women, gold chains, moments of disaster, young teenage boys, environmental blood, and seasonal change. A gun and a voice. A drug of the piercing soul. God is gone within a heart. Plagued with tears of love. Poverty-stricken mothers raising children to die!

A Feeling Such as This

So many tears that fall like rain. Bottled up emotion pours down the drain. Insides burst from pain within, drown by sorrows to no end. The earth is shaken by horrid screams. This is life sometimes, it seems. My eyes will fill, too, each lid. I'll feel the flood. It flows like blood. A feeling such as this.

Cry of the Innocent

Fingers pointing "you're the one" and they cuff you by the gun. It doesn't matter who did the crime. Dead to right, it's your time. There must be a fall guy. Why? Not you! We know you're innocent but the crime belongs to you.

A Pleasant Heart

Shallow graves of the soul, a burdened heart; which won't let go. A time of mourning to relieve this past, to find a pleasant love that last. A heart which seems so far apart that's felt the closeness from the start. A connection of unique kind, a love like ours is hard to find. To grow in peace, unto the end, you're here, you are my friend.

Spiritual Freedom

I looked through the bars but my heart touched the sky. Time and space traveled across the horizon, and God was by my side. My mind began to ponder, a world one day I'd see. A place in Heaven made just for me. Authority from who was set on high but loved in my heart, so why? Should I cry? Peace is God, although I don't see Him. From the day I was born, I've had Spiritual freedom.

Another Day

Some say, "It's just another day." Thunder rolls and the cold winds blow. When it rains it pours. Life changes with seasons. We cry for sunlight more. Troubles come then they go. Winter ceases after the snow. Spring brings a day of cheer. The month of January carries a new year. Autumn leaves tum mindless trees into color; stillness comes before a tornado. Birds seize the water to find food and play. For all of us comes another day.

Perfect Pieces of a Puzzle

I stepped out on my own to find the will of God. I tried to make things happen with every step I trod. I found myself broken while trying to find my way. I hurt others in the process day after day. All the things so similar seemed like this was right, but then it fell to pieces and I couldn't understand why. I try to think of what I did wrong. I pushed my will, for my will is very strong. It all seemed to fit. This just had to be something from God, just for you and me. I made a mistake, oh now sorry! I am. This wasn't meant to be; nor part of His plan. I'm always going to miss you. The little time we had. Because of my failure, I lost a special friend.

Fear and Faith

I could cry tonight knowing you're with another, but I don't have the power or control, you're not my lover. I hold a peace tonight that my God has given. Even though my heart could hurt tonight, my Spirit's risen. Troubles and trials have flown for miles but God's held onto me so many times, I felt I'd break and He was there beside me even when I'd shake. It's love. A river that floods only from above, I only must believe.

You Made Me Strong

You gave me hope all along and the road was a rugged path. To guide me, to direct me, at times you displayed your wrath. Not to hurt but just to heal your child's broken heart. To set my ways and not stray, so the world wouldn't tear me apart. You are my God! I know it's true. You gave me life and peace. You made me strong when days were long and your love has never ceased.

From Hell to My Tranquil Mind

A life spawn of remorse and guilt could've only been created by my undying will. Time after time I wanted to change, but all I did was rearrange. My thoughts were distorted throughout my whole life and I just wanted love, really, not to fight. I was molded from will, I didn't understand. Sometimes I stood still and created a plan. The wrath of hate dwelled within my Soul. Like the tornado, I couldn't let go. I began to destroy everything in my path. I was so annoyed because of my wrath. Hatred and rage were all I knew, I was locked in a cage and almost through. My attitude was cold like the snow on the ground. I felt I was God, nothing would bring me down. Through all the pain and sorrow I caused, my life still remained against my God. I never took time to pause. My will had always kept a bitter taste. Sometimes I wanted freedom from this vicious race. One day I felt in total despair, God picked me up when I started to care. A gradual change began to take place when I changed my will and sought the Master's face.

When My Heart Cries for God

When my father was away, it's because I didn't stay and worship on bended knees. I knew I had to pray that very day so my heart he would see. The problems were my own, my heart began to groan because I needed his guidance and love but I was so weak. As I began to seek the master from above, I began to praise him in worship and thanks for all that He had done. He kept me safe by his loving grace. It was Jesus, God's precious son.

Can We Work It Out?

Last night we had a fight. It wasn't right; my mind was tight. You blamed me, I blamed you. It wasn't true. Words were thrown back and forth; silence touch the ground. You were hurt, I was sore. For once there was no sound. I tried my best to make it right. You wouldn't talk to me. You sat and stared as we rode so I just let you be. I wish I knew what I've done to break your little heart. Please, forgive me. My mind was spun. Can we please find a start? My stomach turns. Because this pain has made you very sad. If we could only just remain, you'd make me very glad. Tell me things that I can do to turn this thing around. If we can talk and see it through. Please! Just make a sound. My mind will speak a dummy's tone and say the wrong things. I forgot to engage my brain, can you still believe in me?

The Highest Praise

Lift up your hands, our savior's here today. Let's glorify our Lord with the highest praise. Jesus is the answer for our crumbling world today. Just lift up your hands as you begin to pray. When you think of His blood and the groan of the cross, remember His love, He died for the lost. Think of each nail as they pierced His hands and feet. Only those who love Him in the clouds He will meet.

I'm Going Home

Is your heart right with God? Do you believe in His throne? I don't know about you, but I'm going home. Do you believe in Heaven when your heart begins to roam? Do you belong to Jesus or are you on your own? What about the cross where Jesus shed his blood? Do you believe in the Son of God and all of His love? Our Lord is coming back. Are you ready to receive the gift of life for all eternity?

Yesterday's Dead and Gone

Yesterday was dark; today is light. Yesterday I collided with life. Surrounded by an army of fear, my world was crushed. The softness of God's voice said hush. God said, "I see your fear. I see every tear. Your life has been tattered and torn since the day you were born. Your voice cries for freedom of this pain, back to a sane mind." To not look behind on the moments of draining power until the Spirit begins to breathe back into your life. I won't dig up the emotional bones of yesterday but I'll accept my reality. For in mind, I'm home today.

Hold onto Your Faith

When it seems there is no way, trust in Jesus and hold onto your faith. He knows your struggles each and every day. But no matter what takes place, you must hold onto your faith. He knows why you hurt. He has known you since birth. He will comfort you in your time of need and He will give you light when there' s no way to see.

Cry of the Angel

He watched over you by the order of God and you were protected with every step you have trod. When you thought you were alone, your Angel was there but you were so unaware. Assigned by the Lord for you, was in his care. Nothing happened by coincidence nor the tear of the guardian that was truly heaven sent, and when he saw you fall, it broke his heart and he would often shed a tear, but would never depart. Your angel was always near.

The Forgotten Past

Dead and buried, this should be. All the pain and misery, living life free. No more suffering. A finished work from the embodiment of a tangled mind; released from the hurt. Accepting fate one day at a time. The grudge and bewilderment are gone forever; no longer mine. And the gut-wrenching sorrow is far from my new life.

He Will Always Be With You

To worry about tomorrow is the deepest sin. God knows your heart, but you pray now and then. Where is your faith? And why do you cry? Can't you believe Jesus is nearby? If he has you in the palm of his hand, why worry? Don't you understand, he has your future and he knows what to do. So trust in him and he will see you through. He is a shield and a buckler, too. There is no need to worry, he will always be with you.

Healing Waters

The spirit flows with healing streams, the peace of God and everything. As the ripples come with every turn over rocks of lessons we truly learn. Channels of love will find the river from healing waters; we neither shake nor quiver.

She Knows

She knows you didn't mean to hurt her She doesn't know your pain no matter how much you cry or how you feel the strain. You wish you could make amends and take back the past, but it never seems to end. It always seems to last. If you could change a thing, what would it be? To release it from, your mind and set this captive free. If she knew how you are today, she might forgive the past and just let it be at last. If she could see your heart and reach beyond your soul, maybe someday she would let it go. If she could see your hurt, your sorrow, and your grief, she might look into your mind where you could find peace.

Free Again

The long road with you and the struggles we've been through, at times we didn't know0 what to do. We tried and tried again, but now we're free with the wind. I still call you my friend. All along the way we drifted apart, but you must know you had a piece of my heart that no one could take away no matter how near or how far. The journey is about time, and space. It's all about God's grace, and maybe one day we will both find our place. A place that no one can see; just a place where we can be free. We will think of each other now and then, but today we are truly free again.

Unrealistic Expectations

Don't throw your heart as far as you can. Your expectations will make up the plan. People will be as they choose but your expectations will cause you to lose. We want people to like us without the games but our expectations still remain the same. We try to love but don't know how, so we hold on to a moment someway somehow. We drive the person completely away when we see them play with another. Still we try to be calm and hide our hurt, but it always blows our cover. They may not mean to break our heart but expectations can rip us apart.

The Power of the Pen

The ink flows to paper by the thoughts only I can see. A spiritual blessing, this time, for me. I can leave today and travel a distant land and look at the waves when they roll against the sand. I'll treasure the moments each time I write and gaze at the stars on a moonlit night. I'll sit on a cliff with a quill in my hand and feel the gentle breeze; the poet that I am.

Life of the Undying

Shall I quit or shall I fight? I will arm myself with peace and gird myself with power upon high. I will find refuge in God. I'll rest by a river and his sweet spirit will breathe through my soul and keep me safe and warm. My eyes will close to surrender, and I will realize that it's just another day.

The conquered Soul

The lame, the smoke, the life, the knife, the cut, and the change. The earth under my feet and the path to freedom. The zone of the skeletal remains of the trudge. The fight, the movement, I must go on. The fiery smolder of the bridge behind. The crisp smell as I turn my head, then I find tranquility from the miles.

A Future of My Own

If I could do life over again, I would change everything. I would change every sin and follow every dream. I'd change my heart from black to red and heal the hidden foe. My mind would be in tune with my spirit for a future of my own. All sin could be forgiven by the Father up above. To rely upon God's only son through the death by His Love.

His Solemn Grace

Stripped of my freedom, I lost it all somehow. Not material possessions. Everything was taken away, never to return right now. The pictures I have and faint memories are all I truly own, and when I think it really hurts me, my mind begins to roam. I lost a love during this time; it was driven to the sea. Two broken hearts, endless waves of pain and misery. I'll start over when I'm out of this dreadful place. But for now I'll pray to God for all His Solemn Grace.

Given to The Wind

Blown through life, pieces of hell. Debris is thrown around. A shattered life like broken glass falling to the ground. Just one moment after the storm, a calmness has arrived. The pain has been "given to the wind" and the burden is left behind.

Safe, Secure, and Warm

When I'm alone with you on a cold winter night, I hold you in my arms with stars shining bright. Love we made before, once has come again. You're always safe and warm and more than just a friend. The love that we share puts a sparkle in our eye. Our hearts are drawn to care, so baby don't you cry. It may seem really long before I make it home, but again we'll be together safe, secure, and warm.

I Yearn for Your Forgiveness

To understand all your pain is something I can't do. I wish I could make it go away, and my love would see you through. I see your tears as you cry. I try to wipe away, but I know you hurt inside each and every day. I make it worse because my mouth never seems to shut, and I feel so distant now, I miss your little touch. Please! Forgive me for what I've done, as human as I am. I ask and beg that you won't run. Just let me hold your hand. My heart is breaking as I write, the tears roll down my face. Can we find a brand new start together in this place? I never planned to fall for you but I truly have. I ask for only one more chance. I feel so very sad. I never thought I would find the woman of my dreams. I pray and pray at this time, you'll please forgive me.

Who Knows?

When I think of you, there's beauty in your eyes. Sparkles of sunshine and the brightest skies. The thought of you grabs my heart and won't let go. My body yearns and cries for your affection My mind races and my spirit pours out the love I feel for you. Your words touch me softly and your grace and charm mold your inner beauty. A fire burns within my soul when I see you smile. Your gentleness and emotional touch grasp every part of my inner being. The likeness of your Spirit and the common bond we share could mean we were meant to be together.

The Key to Your Heart

I hold this key to your heart. I say with only words. I can't describe the way I feel. I feel I must be heard. For you are one of a precious kind that only I will hold. For all my past is left behind and so the memories told. If you let me just come in, I'll be your friend for life. I'll help you in your time of need and help you not to cry. Don t think of all the other ones, or who I had before. If you give me just one chance, I'll love you even more. I can't believe that we've just met, my life has changed so much. I've begun to write again with that special touch. Before you came, my words were dead. I couldn't write a thing. But now I know you are here and this is not a dream. You tend to brighten up my day with all you say and do, with all your loving caring ways. You make my dreams come true. I hope that you don't take this wrong, I know we're only friends. But if you let me come along, we'll see how this will end!

You're A Child of God

A child of God, you'll always be. Your love for Jesus has set you free. When man condemns and brings you down, just think of the Cross where He was bound. Yes, it's true. They laughed at Him, they scorned Him, and beat Him because of our sin. For He must know all our pain. For haters and backbiters, the lamb was slain. God's love for you will never change, and in His heart you'll always remain.

The Playing Field

Three strikes you're out. You've been there before, heard the slamming door. The demon bit you again You thought he was your friend. One time you received a hug. It's called the devil's drug. Meth and mayhem are their names, and with you it's the deadly game. You try to battle when the curve ball is thrown. But out on the field, you're sure to stand alone.

A Pillar of Fire

A blazing fire, a crippling disease, a cry for the strong, a tortured brain will lift from the fog and peace will be within. A touch of a hand will carry the map, direction, and footsteps to trod. I'll deliver a message to this new one, and leave the rest to God. Their thinking must change the old beaten path to live in the now and to be saved by the wrath. To awaken each day, your new place is here. Hold fast to the steps; let them dry up your tears.

Shadows in the Evening

As the sun goes down not even a sound, just the whistling of the breeze. The day is gone and night has come. The sun has been pleased. Smiles of laughter filled the afternoon and cheerfulness in the air. Winds of silence have come again. The heart of life is there. All the beauty of the Earth is really the only reason. We enter our homes, some are alone, and the shadows are in the evening.

A Hungry Soul

I used to feed the little birds. They played outside my door. Then I watched them fly away with the wind. They would soar. I felt like them in a sort of way, because God created me, too. The multicolor the birds displayed, each blend and hue. The spirit within them, how could it be? They're given life and the skies are free. Just like the Hungry Soul I have for more of Jesus to feed the spirit sad.

The Master of the Clouds

Today, is my father above? I feel safe in His love. I know I'm His child. I know I was wild but have the spirit of a dove. This rushing mighty wind inside fills my every being. I know He's there. I know He cares even though I don't see Him. Engulfed by Angels, protected every day, I will be as long as my Father sees me pray.

In The Reaper's Hand

I'm having fun. I'm under the gun. I really like the edge, but cold blood runs through my veins. The next day I dread. Last night was cool but I was a fool chasing the dragon. I vow no more today. I'm on the wagon to stay. The drugs hammer my brain, I'm going insane. Another fix goes something like this. I need to feel better. My clothes are tom. I was warned. I knew it was now or never.

My Spirit Cries

Today, I'm free. I know who I am. Today I care about my fellow man. Tears of joy fill my eyes. I see God's creatures nearby. Thank you, God, for my freedom, for this season, a season of joy; the freshness of your Spirit as it enters my soul. To love is my goal. Today I cry tears of joy. The sadness has left this little boy.

An Empty World

When we have run a vicious race and feel our heart has been misplaced. We'll grab and hold on to anything because we've lost the future's dream. Our will is strong but even still our days are long as we climb the hill. If we could find the wayward path, the spirit of God would cease our wrath. Although our heart knows the way, the sinner's prayer has gone astray.

Spirit of the Laboring Crush

From the choices we've made, gripped the wretched look. Feeling of the numb, and our bones have weakened. We wronged others, but to make it right, is to ask for the unforgiven. The eye, the train of thought, and change surmounted by prayer and lay to rest the damage.

The Calmness of the Earth

Life is silent today, I see. I see the stillness of the trees. The ground doesn't move. The sky is the background of this painted scene. To you this may be just words but I see the calmness of the Earth.

Easter

Easter is the time of year when bunnies bring us cheer. Children smile for a while as we hold them dear. Baskets are filled with candy and eggs are hidden behind a tree. Laughter shared with family and friends, and true love we see. Happy times for every child when they receive their gift. But what about the true delight when Jesus died to live?

The Breath of Life

The breath from his nostrils He created a man, and from the dust of the ground God made him stand. His descendent was Noah, a righteous man of God, who built an ark to save his family from the flood. The wrath of God made the waters swell, but then he sent Jesus to save us from hell. There are many who don't believe, and there will come a time when their souls will grieve. The point of the rapture is what matters most; the Father, Son and Holy Ghost.

The Forgotten Past

Dead and buried, this should be; forgotten moments of pain and misery. Living life free; no more suffering. A finished work having the embodiment of a tangled mind. Accepting fate. The grudge of bewilderment gone forever, the gut-wrenching sorrow given to life, and the forgiveness of a foe.

The Shepherd's Voice

I heard a cry throughout the night and my sheep was lost in terrible fright. I saw a tear run down its eye. When the darkness came and the storm blew, my little one prayed and I came to its rescue. Only my child can hear my voice, and in times of trouble they shall rejoice. For I am Jesus. I am the king. The true son of God who is everything.

Beyond the Sun

On a bright sunny day, I looked at the sky. I tried to look beyond. I wanted to find Heaven far away. I was seeking God's Son. I knew He was there. He's high on a throne. So I began to stare as I stood there all alone. From what I could see, there was truth in my mind. I read about this place time after time. The splendor above the colors and light, from my Lord and Savior, Heaven was bright. I saw the Angels about the throne, giving glory to God and now I'm not alone. There were twenty-four Elders praising Jesus and His name, and since I had this happen, I've never been the same.

He left the Throne

I was plagued by fear, felt so alone. But my Lord ran to me; I was a lost sheep. I started to pray but Jesus saw my pain. I was so hurt inside and started to cry. Then he called my name. I knew he was nearby. I was free from the grip of life, and I've never been the same. He bathed me in love and I found my way to heaven the day I was saved and in his love I remain.

A Divine Purpose

Don't ask me why I'm still here, but God has a plan for me. Why should I fear? Or shed a tear? Because peace and joy are coming. Waves of splendor shall encompass my being, and God knows the reason although I don't see him. My flesh and form still has life; a divine purpose will come in time.

I'm Just Me

I'm feeling the air with the presence of God and the love he has for me. The wind of the spirit blows through my heart, and today I know I'm free. I'm now on a spiritual plane. Before I didn't see. But today I know God loves me, and I love that I'm just me.

The Passionate Writer

When I choose my quill and dip it in the ink, my heart begins to swell as my mind begins to think. My Spirit becomes overwhelmed as I travel around the world. You see, I'm a poet. I have a story to tell. My words, they have meaning to which there is no end. I use my imagination like I'm talking to a friend. They say I'm a deep person from the words that fill my heart for I'm the passionate writer. I know just where to start. As my words flow to paper, I begin to feel. The keys of the mystery and the magic becomes real. Fantasies and experiences, and the joy that I find. I'm a passionate writer. Yes, this is true! I lay my quill to the ink for the love I have for you.

Torn

Evil has descended upon me. I'm full of hate. A gray day. Depression has attacked my mind, no peace to find. I've been left behind A struggle within. Not my friend, this is not the end. I'm a survivor, I'll fight for my serenity to bring light to my reality.

Depression

A blocked mind, never-ending thoughts, an alliance of pain. Misused emotion bottled up inside but no place to hide, only strain. Release of a deadened soul is what I crave. Nothing seems to matter. A heart that's angry for the state it's in you. Just can't win so the depression stays within.

When Love Hurts

Rain has descended to my eyes. Pain has caused the flow. Thinking of all I left behind, darkness created for reasons I didn't know why. Broken fellowship with a loved one. Tears of forgiveness fall in spurts. A person vanishes from your life. When love hurts Angels cry, but power sustains us from within. Even though we can't say what we feel to this friend.

A Distant Land

Last night I had a dream about a place far away. Streams of blue oceans, dolphins at play. Coconut trees graced the shore line. Islands sprung with volcanoes in the background. A flavor with the scent of love from the fragrance of this natural distant land, and beaches with white grains of sand as we hold each other's hands.

Watching the Sun

The sun looked on this morning and I gazed into His eyes. Bright, shining, and glowing winds of Spring produced Heavenly skies. The stillness of the clouds of orange and blue design. Pierced through the horizon and the sun would see the Earth one more time. Over the trees beyond the mountains, the ocean awakes. The candle is lit. Waters crash the shore and the gulls prey at the beach.

God's Sweet Peace

Are you a man when you walk away? Does your heart ache while you pray? It's in our flesh to want to fight. Are we like Jesus every day and every night? I know what it was like before you were saved. But what is more important, His word or an early grave?

A Brighter Day Ahead

Life is full of many things; clouds, silver linings, bountiful dreams. Rain will fall the wind must blow but a brighter day is coming. As we trudge alone, don't fear perilous times of pain, It's only for a moment, so we must remain.

The Other Side of Heaven

I continued to pray and wait for Him so I could leave in flight. I knew that He would take me home "like a thief in the night." I pondered His coming and looked at the sky, and my tears began to run. Then I saw Jesus in the clouds nearby, as bright as the sun. He called my name and I came to Him and then I held His hand. He dried my tears when He looked in my eyes and He took me to the promised land.

Judge Me Not!

Pointing fingers round and round, casting curses, spells abound. You try to destroy the inner me, but lack the power because I'm free. Yes, I've sinned and so have you. Are you any better? What did you do? Judge me not, it's not your place. Look in the mirror at your saddened face.

I'm Your Ego

I'm better than you, so I think. I must believe I'm cruel and mean. I'll stick my nose in the air. To hell with people, I don't care. I'm a glutton for attention, as you can see. My vanity and power is the real me. I'll use you and abuse you until I'm done, because stroking my ego is where I have fun. I'll not care who I crunch, I'll eat people every day for lunch. I'm proud and I'm poised because I think I'm full of power. I'll drain you and defeat you until you are devoured. I'm arrogant, grandiose, and vanity is a must. If you step on my toes, you've sure to make me cuss. I'm selfish, mean, self-centered to the extreme. Your feelings are feathers that I'll blow away with the wind. When we meet, are you ready to cry? Because when we're found out, we will die inside.

Torture Because of my Sin

You toil with my brain like putty in your hands. Laughter, the look of a demon, a destroyer of some kind, I don't understand. Bent on removing the blood from your prey. Is that all you think of each day? I cry to God for relief. He sits with folded hands, motionless. Tears on his face, this has to be.

The Plea

I beg of you to let me out. I've paid enough, there is no doubt. Torment of the continuum, life in a dormant state, frozen fear, a holocaust of painful memories, unspoken language: just thoughts in my brain. Surrender to my accuser. Don't pass judgment on me, I beg of you, please! Let me go free.

I Sat Alone

I sat alone, just time to think about my life, what did it mean? No key, no dimension through walls. Concrete and steel, locked in time. Strangers who serve with evil eyes. Mind games from devils and demons cross my path every day. I need my freedom.

The Flame

Burned by life, the flames were hot and smoldering ashes I haven't forgot. Bits and pieces of my life danced in the air. Freely flown I didn't care. The wind changed, the fire spread. Consumed by flames, my heart was dead. My soul ascended to its place. The aftermath, my past erased.

The Scroll

A rolled up scroll beside my bed. A sleepless night and thoughts that bled. No peace within and bound with fear, but the rolled up scroll I hold dear. Within the scroll were words of truth. My fears would die and leave me soon. For the rolled up scroll was life ahead. For the one that planned it on a Cross He had bled.

I Love Your Tender Touch

You stood by me through thick and thin. You have always been my friend. Our love was placed in Heaven back then. Two hearts bound together, became one. We stood the stormy weather and even had some fun. We've been through so much, but I hunger for your soft, tender touch. Thinking of you, oh! How precious you are. Your eyes are like diamonds within the brightest star.

A Touch from Your Nail-Scarred Hand
What Did I Ever Do to Deserve Thee?

What did I ever do to deserve thee? With the grace that you've given to me. You suffered on a cross and died upon Calvary's tree. Why did you ever love me? I failed you in every way. Was it me that should've been there? I didn't take your place. They drove the nails so deeply and pierced your bleeding side. You gave yourself to your father, took one breath and died. Jesus, why did you love me? And Jesus, why did you care? I stood as you prayed in the garden that day and no one to help you anywhere. Why did you carry my burden? You struggled to reach the hill. I know in my heart for certain, you were doing your father's will. I stood at the place where they laid you and stared at the blood-drenched shroud. I saw where your body was broken, I had to leave you for now. Today I know you're in heaven and you bore my cross in pain. Now standing in the garden, I see the tears that remain. I know that you'll come for your children and you'll meet them in the air. I just want to say, I'm sorry! You wore my sins back there. Just a touch from your nail-scarred hand.

When Dreams Come True

When dreams come true, you find that love and it begins to show. A thought, a perception of time, you truly know and onward you go. You pray with hope and your mind is free. Like the ocean breeze, only your dream can see. A thought enters your mind; so close yet so far away. But you know you will have your dream someday. In God's time and you must know that the future is in his hand. At the end of the quest, you will finally begin to understand.

The Trinity

Never-ending love, the cross, the dove, heaven above. The shield of life, the protector in the night. The power that brings out the best in you, the guide. And so your heart comes to you. When you know that, it will see you through.

"Daily Points to Ponder"

Every living Human Being is God's handiwork, who am
    I to judge what God has placed on this Earth?
The dark past can be changed into light.
I need to look at life as it was intended; to keep an
    open mind and spread love not hate.
The way of the soul is to believe in Jesus Christ, God's Son.
I must express myself with spiritual power instead of throw-
    ing my weight around with self-defeating behavior.
To harm another is to sharpen the sword and pierce the heart. I
    will begin to look at all God's Creation as Precious Gems
    to hold fast to. A resentment is to destroy one's own soul.
    To talk about another is to sever a heart with hate.
To heal the mind is to heal the spirit.
To crush the heart is to devour the spirit.
The fragrance of serenity is peace, joy, and happiness.
Love is a treasure beyond imagination.
Fantasies are dreams and dreams are fanta-
    sies. Love makes them come true.
Peace and harmony multiply care for the wounded.
What is important today is the admiration of life.
I've made volumes of mistakes but I'm trying to improve the book.
After a rain, I'll gaze upon the bow placed in the clouds.

The Spirit Within

The soul, the mind, the love, and the spirit within. The trinity, the peace, the joy, you're free again. Pain is gone and given to the wind. You have a new song, it plays again and again. Serenity given to prayer, and kindness you show everywhere, and today your spirit is your friend.

In Time of War

We didn't know the time would come that we would be apart. Holding each other and having fun were spoken in our heart. We loved so long and made it strong, this bond could never end. I went off to war to settle a score; for my Country I had to win. Think of me where you are, I'm coming back some day. I will be there waiting for you when I come back home to stay. Embrace me in your heart and mind, it's only for a while. Keep the faith, cradle our love, and hold it with a smile. Don't let the tears that you cry cave your little heart. I'm sorry that I said goodbye. I'm sorry we had to part.

A War-Torn Soldier

Rugged in battle, the soldier fought a war. He couldn't win alone. He's been so distraught. He wished that it would end. From the blood that's shed each day, a torn soldier continues to pray and the soldier wishes he had a friend today.

The Star Light Moon

As we dance in the shadows with our love, it's evening in the night of June. Only the two of us hold this love in our hearts beneath the starlit moon. Glistening candles of the flickering wick is true of all we see. Caring and sharing, holding each other; memories that forever will be.

Take This Memory from Me, Lord

Take this memory from me Lord, no longer remembered again. Pain and suffering, all that sin, lay them in the Sea. Help me, please, Lord set me free. Take the chains that bound my heart and help me to breathe again. Forgive me for the pain I caused; another's sorrow I pause. I'll give thanks to the bridge burned behind for there's a new tomorrow.

Buried in the Past

Haunting memories seem to always last but only God can bury the past. Thoughts of troubled times never go away but God can take them today. Just let it go and forever it will be. Jesus knows and He will set you free. It's only for a season but stays within your mind. Just let it go and leave your past behind

Close to the Grave

Pen and paper are all I have, and a story of life that I once lived but became very sad. At age thirteen I accepted The Lord but I just couldn't fathom any of His Word. Kids made fun of the way I looked and I began to believe them when I shook. I felt The Hand of God walk away from me when I turned away from Calvary's tree. Life really got crazy when I went to jail but I turned my back on Jesus and was caged in hell. I remember the day on my way to the grave when I was shackled and bound. No hope could I say. The officers led me through the fences and razor wire. I didn't know what to do, my heart was on fire. You see, when you sin against God and you walk away, the devil will take you close to the grave and you will die if you are not saved.

The Song of Years

I wait for the day my freedom will say it's time for me to go home, but until then I'll find peace within and know I'm not alone. God really cares. He's always there when I need to hold His hand. I must always trust in Him although I don't understand. It will be alright. He tells me at night through His loving spirit. He holds me with care. The Angels are aware when I cry those tears. It won't be long, one of these days I'll sing the song of years. I'll put it in the past. The days will be over at last, and all my horrid fears.

Grandmother

Words can't describe the love I feel for you. My heart cries with blessings for all you say and do. Your cheerful smile is shown with grace from within, Grandma. Now I'm grown and you know where I've been. You're wise and understanding when I talk to you. Although times are hard you still tell me what to do. If I just had a moment to take you to a place, we'd hold hands together and kneel down and pray.

The Mind of a Jealous Heart

Don't they care about your success? They love to bring you down. Don't you wish they would lay to rest their feelings without a sound? Do they get pleasure scoffing at you when they see your treasure and your dream coming true? They do what they do. They build themselves up to make you feel less, but all you want for them is the very best.

Strangled by Love

You're only a memory. We're never again to touch. I never realized I loved you so much. A memory you'll be through all my given days. A treasure I could see with your special ways. A friendship that we shared is now dead and gone. When you're strangled by love, it's such a bitter song. When my heart cries out for that gentle kiss, it's you my precious love that I miss. We had our ups and downs and wrestled with our words. At times things were silent but then we'd both be heard. It wasn't meant to be. It came from up above. But as you can clearly see, I'm strangled by your love.

The Mirror in the Brook
Written by Mark Hamilton

As I sat on the bank, as I had peace in my heart,
My life was so serene, cause the night before I
    saw a brook, and it was in a dream.
The key to my life was in this brook, as I watched the water flow.
The spirit of god and the future ahead is something I did not know.
He laid my heart upon a rock, for my heart was in his care.
The spirit of God was all around and I knew that he was there.
He reached and took me by the hand and walked me to the edge,
He said, "Son, I hope you understand, for you this is my pledge
Try to keep your faith in me; I'll help you all I can.
I will even set you free, if you can understand.
My precious son gave his life for all that I had made.
My heart broke, and I burst in tears, as they laid him in the grave.
So when you see the water flow, remember just one thing, I
    am still the Lord of Hosts, and this is not a dream. "

Book Cover
"The Breadth of Life"

Try to put a price on serenity and you will be shortchanged
If you don't roll with the punches, the punches will roll with you
Keep the peace, so the peace will keep you
     Learn to love and love to learn
If it's in your heart, it's in your mind
To add stress to your life means to add pressure to yourself
Realistic goals are goals already set, It's called common sense
Anger should be handled with your brain not your brawn
To know God is to know peace and to have
     no God is to have no peace
Reach for the stars and the stars will reach for you

The Captain

On a dark stormy night during the roughest sea, no one was there but the captain and me. The fire burned within me, the fear made me shake. The master calmed my heart and his hand I did take. The waves began to roll, turn my life upside down, and the captain held me close to the hem of his gown. The winds blew heavy, so heavy in my mind. But the captain held me close and said, "Child, you'll be fine." I couldn't see the waves coming so high but the captain steered my vessel all through the night. I asked the captain, "Why the rough waves? Wasn't life hard enough from our endless days?" The captain paused and thought of what I had said, then I looked in his eyes and saw how he had bled. Just for a moment I began to cry. I thought of the cross and how the captain died.

The Field of Roses

I walked through the roses stained in crimson red, and remembered the cross and how our Savior bled. The blood had caressed and flooded my feet and I stepped on a thorn that I didn't see. The weight held me down as I walked through the field and the pain was so great. I remembered the hill. There were so many roses, I felt so lost. I thought about Jesus and I remembered the cross.

A Lost Loved One

I'm sorry that you went away. You soar above the clouds. I hope and pray we'll meet someday but we can't for now. You have a place in my heart that I will always keep.

It's very hard to know you're gone but I know that you're at peace. The angels took you from us all; we couldn't understand but God takes us great and small for it's written in his plan. It doesn't stop the tears we've shed nor does it stop our grief but we know you are there, so now we can sleep. The only thing we hold onto was what we had before. But I always know, as days go by, I love you even more.

The Weight

Life's problems are rough, at times very tough when we don't know our fate. We didn't carry the cross, we didn't pay the cost, nor did we walk through the gate. We weren't whipped; we didn't trip. He carried our sin that day. His blood fell in streams along with His screams; He felt love not hate. We should have been there. Do we really care what happened on that day? For Jesus died. He was crucified for all the sin we'd display. When we think of ourselves and the bitter hell which seems to plaque our mind, do we think of the Cross and how He died for the lost? Do we think of that time? On that horrid day our King did say, "Father, where are you?" God turned His head as Jesus bled, said, "Son it's almost through." When they took him down there wasn't a sound, the blood continued to fall. His body ripped in shreds, a crown upon his head for Jesus loved us All.

Frailty of Emotion

Longing for love, acceptance, and peace, belonging to one who seeks. To find the abundance of inner strength and to conquer what's beneath. To look inside a tainted heart and broken from life's dream, and to end it all from the start without really seeing. The pride of all to know yourself comes with much devotion, and to break the chains within the spell and the frailty of emotion.

From the Cross to Prison and Back "Broken Dreams, the Mended Soul"

With all the ego and pride, I learned to live my way. I blamed it all on someone else until that very day. Freedom lost, decisions made, the court took their stand. My life was in the system but still was in God's hand. Dungeons of evil and the wicked men spoke. With thoughts of deception, their spirit was no joke. Tamed as an animal tranquilized with chains. I cried to the Lord, he told me "just remain." I sought out the past from the place I once prayed. When I accepted Jesus, a young boy had things to say. With all the fear my mind began to change. I found my way back to the cross, and I've never been the same.

If You Bury Me, I Shall Live

A frozen cloud and no drop of rain. Problems have taken my breath. Negative emotions travel distant lands and won't capture one grain of sand. I will fight, I will forgive. I will love and I will live. I will change to a much better man, but the cold shall come again. Although I was buried, today I will live.

Close to the Sun

The future is bright but I'm under the gun. Savage winds rip and tear me to pieces. Storms of grief, a sparkling star, then a crash of thunder. The grind of the fallen mountain as my voice cries out in pain.

Pieces of a Bleeding Heart

Purged to look back as I feel my heart drip tears of red as it cries. Wish it could mend; to this there is no end. Filled with blood, a mind of its own. Open or closed is its choice.

Emotional twists, my heart feels as it thinks. A message is sent to build a wall of preservation. Experiencing hurt no more. A knight or princess appears, sees the tears by my wounded voice. The knight or princess wants to understand but can't possibly feel the burning. Afraid to trust again and my heart lays dormant but has thoughts of hope. A gift is brought by a caring soul but this heart has had too much rain, too many blows.

Yesterday Is Dead and Gone

Yesterday was dark, today is light. I collided with life. Surrounded by an army of fear, my world was crushed. The softness of God's voice said hush. God said, "I see your fear. I see every tear. Your life has been tattered and torn since the day you were born. Your voice cries for freedom of this pain, back to a sane mind." To not look behind on the moments of draining power until the Spirit begins to breathe back into your life. I won't dig up the emotional bones of yesterday, but I'll accept my reality. For in mind, I'm home today.

Can You Hear Me?

My heart cries out for someone near just to hold my hand. So I'll begin to shed a tear and only want a friend. To laugh and talk and joke around. Will someone break the ice? To share a different point of view no matter who is right. To talk about all the things that make our life worthwhile. To look into each other's eyes and hold them with a smile. To walk along a sandy beach as the water touches our toes. To see the moonlit sky and reach beyond our inner soul. As the night begins to fall and the stars begin to shine, we begin to understand a love that's so alive. A fire starts, begins to burn into our loving ways. A romance now forevermore through all our given days. We gaze across the ocean and take an endless flight. For we found love with all emotion, and we know it's right.

I Can't Save the World

Power lies only in my God; the secrets that he holds. He has a plan that's just for me. Others have their own. What about the stone heads that want their own way and the deadly game they play day after day? It's not for me to figure out the path others should take, and it's not for me to decide the life that they create.

Soft Moments

Delivered by Angels' wings, you came to me with one of an understanding mind to give me peace which is kind. You show me love and pray with me. A risk for your own inner peace. A loving Spirit, a tender heart. I cling to you and want you in my arms. Last night I had a dream fate would have its way. One touch from your lips; said, "Honey, it will be okay." Raiment of your golden hair, eyes of blue. A captured moment of admiration. A magic touch when we make love, a tame sentiment of tenderness fused together in our nakedness, a passionate kiss goodnight. Peace sanctified by a sweet Spirit and loving hope, I'll hold you next to me. A precious moment in time.

The Haven of Death

At the altar we pray for peace. We think of our soldiers that the fighting will cease. Their minds are broken from this bitter war. Their lives are so empty; they die by the sword. The sword is the power of the Generals within to kill and devour an army of men. No love, no solace, this desolate place could only be conquered by God's solemn grace.

The Trials of Life

The trials of life are for us to grow. To be Spiritually sound is our ultimate goal. To live our journey, which is good for us, and to love all is truly a must. Life is full of ups and downs. We cry time after time, but when our heart beats to this sound, we know that we'll be fine.

The Gift

On Christmas morn, I looked under the tree. Times were hard, no present for me. Mother and Dad did the best they could. Beaten by pain wasn't too good. The crops in the field weren't much this year. So here we go, without Christmas cheer. The other kids had plenty of fun. Johnny my neighbor got a new BB gun. With others, trees, ornaments and gifts. I hurt inside for a spiritual lift. All at once, God spoke to me, "Son, I see your cry. Listen, it's me. I know you want like other kids, but wasn't my birth truly the best gift?"

New Beginnings

The sun, the flowers, the seasons of rain. A future of life that still remains. Darkness overcome by love and joy. Peace within every little girl and boy. Visions of laughter and brightness ahead. Magic from a book that has never been read.

Stolen

From the departure of endless seas, waves from the past to the mind received. Taken from the heart, a barren life. Brought with an attitude that cut like a knife. Carved in the days from where it has begun, hoping for an answer from the love of someone. Missing the laughter, the joy, and the peace, my treasure was taken; it was stolen from me.

I Believe

I believe the cross was made for Jesus for the souls He would save. To minister in love, God's son was slain. He endured hours of horrific pain. His blood trickled as the last drop fell when He conquered demons at the gates of hell. Remember being more than just wood, the Cross held our King on the hill where it stood. The sins of the world bludgeoned His heart. He would cry and scream while his flesh ripped apart.

Rumors

People spread lies about the truth. What they believe makes others feel blue. Only God saw all that was done but they stand to judge. They feel superior, a loaded gun. Do they know how we've bled? Our hearts will feel anger and pain until death. Talebearers, gossipers, they stand in deceit to drain our love and kill us with grief. What do we do with people like this who steal our joy, our hope, and our bliss?

Death of a Servant

My mind is full of emotional twists. My heart is bent and burned. Love is bled out of my flesh, for my soul changed and turned. Where's the love God has for me? If I'm a prisoner, please set me free! You have a plan, I must believe. It's not to just exist. Please straighten my mind before I die from life's emotional twists.

Held by Faith

Increasing joy in the arms of God, to trust and honor all His love. Receiving blessings of the day through perseverance when I pray, I hold the Cross by the truth. For his blood was shed for me, too. The streams of pain that Jesus felt before He pulled the keys from hell! We're held by faith and by His word, we do His will or die by the sword. When Satan orchestrates an attack on us, we cling to the Father watching from above.

His Abundant Love

His arms will reach around your heart when life has thrown you and torn you apart. He'll engulf and carry you with his love for he made the angels from the stars above. His love is abundant. He died on the cross and all of his blood was shed for the lost. He could've let us die, and he could've let us fall, but he gave his life for the pain of us all.

If I Could Leave the Earth

If I could leave the earth, I would fly through the sky. I'm sure I would find heaven somewhere nearby. Who really knows about this magical place? Only Jesus by the throne from his solemn grace. We are told about streets of gold and of angels and elders; the Bible told us so. We're told there are gates of pearl and a mansion for us. What about our loved ones who have come and gone? Do they sit by the angels while they play their songs? I know they praise God for all that he has made. The love of the Father and the Son that he gave. If I could leave the earth, I would fly through the sky.

Prayers of Stone

I bow down before him and try to seek his face. He must be hiding because of my lack of song and praise. He's a jealous **God**. It's written in the word. He'll only reveal himself when you worship and you serve. We know it's not a feeling when we bow before the Lord. We've only us to blame when we don't read His word. We often cry in pain and wonder if He hears; if our prayers are in vain. It only brings Him tears. Pray for the sinner, the homeless, and the lost. For Jesus shed his blood and He paid the cost. Remember when you pray and think that you're alone, God will hear your prayers if your spirit isn't stone.

Forgiveness

How many we've hurt? How many we've scorned? How much has been lost? How much has been torn? We bring terror to our minds, know just what we have done. Left people behind while we were having fun. We come to a road where we must endure, and the pain and hurt will come for sure. It's time to make that amend before they die, and no longer are your friend. Let's clear our minds, let's think of what's best. A word or I'm sorry will leave a soul to rest.

Power is strong in wrong ways, but forgiving a foe can brighten our days. A grudge is bleak, a broken heart bad, forgiveness held in makes one very sad.

Faith

Life makes us tremble when burdened by the fight. Faith is lessened with time. As we began to fear the future ahead, we feel we're losing our mind. The Earth is his footstool; the power is in his hand. His marker is creation and his breath in every man. So why do we fear when there seems to be no end? For the master is near again and again.

The Eye of the Storm

Dear Father above, you're the Eye of the storm. You've known me well since the day I was born. When the whirlwinds came, you gave me peace within. Although I had failed you from the blood of my sin. I saw no way out for what I had done, but I still believed I was your son. My mind was thrown; I was turned all around. You held me close when I fell to the ground. I suffered much grief from what I had caused, but soon found relief and remembered the cross. I can't say it's over because the worst is yet to come. You'll be in the courtroom until the victory's won. Although I won't see you, you'll be holding my hand, as well as the Judge before I take the stand. How could I have known the web that I spun? It's only by grace, I didn't leave and run. Fear used to be my emotional toll, but facing recovery will help me reach my goal. A few hours now, I'll take the drive. I'll meet the Judge and Jury inside. I still believe I'll be safe and warm because God I know you'll hold me in the eye of the storm.

The Love of God

The love of God is so serene, he calms my heart when I dream so bent and twisted. Sometimes I am the love of God who comes from His Lamb. I'm His child; will always be. For the love of God has set me free.

My Loving Father

Good morning! Lord, how are you? From your throne of Grace, you'll see me through! You know my heart. Why should I fret with all my frailties? You still love me. From this winding road you've given me peace, and my love for you shall never cease! Oh! What a pleasure to know you're above. Oh! What a treasure, it's your undying love. Although I stumble and I fall, your grace will sustain me through it all!

We Found Love

When birds sing and flowers bloom, love smiles on me and you. Just a walk in the park while we're holding hands is the joy of life, and isn't it grand? As the sun shines on us both, love really happens and we know there's hope. For God gave us this precious gift; to love and be loved is a special lift. When we share our thoughts and prayers, we know that our love will always be there. Is it possible there is fate? When love shows up we can't be late. Through all the times we loved but didn't, we burrowed pains into our hearts. With all the effort that we made, our minds were ripped apart. God has a clock that we don't understand. When the time is right, we'll lay in the sand. We'll cling to each other and behold the warmth. We will love each other till death do us part. We tend to run a vicious race because we lose sight of God's grace. He knows what is best and sometimes we're put to the test. Our will leads us today but we really know who has the last say if it's meant for me and you. There's nothing truly God won't do. No man, woman, child, or beast can ever destroy our love or peace. For if it's written in the stars, God will take us very far. I didn't plan the life I've lived, nor did I know then. You're the flower that I see, my very special friend.

The Prince of Heaven

A far away land, a magical place, a throne of grace. Angels guard him by the sword. Clothed in white raiment, He is our Lord. He admires his kingdom from heaven above, and cares for his children with all of his love. The prince of heaven who was once slain, and the lamb of God still remains. He sits above the circle of the earth; He's our savior and our king. For it's written in his word. How can one not believe? That Jesus died on Calvary.

The Poet That I am

My ink flows to paper by the thoughts I conceive, and frees my mind and all that's within me. I can leave today and travel a distant land, and look at the waves as they roll against the sand. I'll treasure the moment each time I write and gaze at the stars on a moonlit night. I'll sit on a cliff with my quill in hand and feel the gentle breeze; the poet that I am.

His Unconditional Love

Jesus, I've told you I'm sorry! I just can't count the times. No matter how much I've hurt you, you've always been by my side. Your love is full of compassion, your peace and serenity. You shed your blood on the cross. It's true you died for me. I've been imperfect so many times, and yes I was born in sin. But you still loved me and I don't know why! Your spirit never left me then. When I think of you all the time, I remember the cross and the blood, and when I see the bluest sky I feel your unconditional love.

When My Heart Cries for God

When my father was away, it's because I didn't stay and worship on bended knees. I knew I had to pray that very day so my heart he would see. The problems were my own, my heart began to groan because I needed his guidance and love but I was so weak. As I began to seek the master from above, I began to praise him in worship and thanks for all that he had done. He kept me safe by his loving grace. It was Jesus, God's precious son.

My Serenity is Love

I cried, oh I cried rivers of tears. My heart was broken for so many years. I leaned on Jesus to see me through until I lost my faith and promise, too! Today I believe in this power, the power of Almighty God. For He's here with me through every step I've trod. My life had no meaning and my mind was a barren land. I'd say it would be hard for people to understand. But the more I strive to be happy, joyous, and free, the more I believe in Jesus who died on Calvary.

Today I have peace and my serenity is love.

The Cross I Have to Bare

Blood drops were falling; tears fell like water. Wounds cried out and pain burned him on the inside. The burden of my life was weighed by his stripes. Innocent but yet a prisoner. The filthy stench, the rejection, the embarrassment, a lonely place. No end, no light. Darkness encircled by fear. You knew by his face, drenched flesh, physical enthusiasm, broken bones, a torn garment, hope passed away. A grieving mother, her baby was dying that day, helpless and powerless over evil. Laughter and humiliation, eyelids weak and closed. It should've been me that hung on that tree. All my sin stained his robe.

Treasure in a Peril

Deep inside the Spirit Sea, encased in love until it's free. Guarded from the past and it won't let you in; always protected until you are a friend. The closer you get the more it draws away. It must be pursued slowly, yours to take. A dream for a child, with every boy and girl. For in every one of us lies a treasure in a pearl.

If I could Go to Heaven

If I could go to Heaven, I'd leave here today. I would pray to the Lord that my soul he would take. In a twinkling of an eye, I could be with him and fellowship with Jesus, and time would never end.

Until the Very End

This crisis came when my body was weak. I didn't have a clue about my defeat. My mind trembled with fear and despair. I searched for God and he was there. My hurt began to flood my being. I called on the master although I couldn't see him. God saw me as his child. I walked up to him and he held me for a while. He said, "Son, I've loved you before and because you are mine, I love you even more." His arms covered me with Angels' wings and I began to cry because of everything. He dried the tears from my face and said, "Son, I'm here for you. I love you with grace. I knew you then and I know you now. I feel your pain and your hurt. It's gotten you somehow. But from the dust and the day you were born, my heart would break when I knew yours had torn. But always remember one special thing, I'm your heavenly father until the very end."

The Land of Entanglement

I spun a web with no escape. Through all the strands, there was no way. It was in my head I know it's true. I couldn't see because of you. I chose to let you play this game. To enter my mind and drive me insane. I won't let you take my life or my peace. You're not worth it, you're just a disease. I tried to help you in every way but you betrayed me so please go away.

Jesus, You're the Answer

Mighty Lord Jesus, please! Hear my cry. I know you're with me. I know you're nearby. Please! Dry my tears. Oh, would you please? By your nail-scarred hands with holes meant for me. Please, touch my heart with your love and warmth, and fill my Spirit from a heart that's torn. When my pain begins, you feel it too. Tears flood your eyes but you know just what to do. You'll pick me up and hold me tight. You're the answer to my prayers every day and every night. When hard times come, as they often do, I know you're the answer and you'll see me through.

God's Gift
(A Special One's for Me)

You may say you're not much. What is there to give? I see no talent in myself. For what purpose do I live? I struggle always from day to day, trying to find my way. I know a place just for me given by His grace. I oft complain to myself, there must be more to life. But all I find is obstacles. It seems there's always strife. In his words I know it's true, I have gifts and talents, too. If I look within my mind I'd be surprised of the things I'd find. For God gave us all these gifts for all of us to see, and these gifts you may have but a special one's for me.

The Rapture Has Come

Today I've ascended through the clouds above. I'm with Jesus, I flew with the doves. I can't look back now; my life has begun. The Earth was my dressing room; a vapor has come. Hey, look there's the lamb! I can see his nailed-scarred hands. Hey, look it's David the King! I'm so amazed with the angels' wings.

The Dream

An Angel came before me while I was fast asleep. He said because of my sins, what I sowed I'd also reap. I didn't know the Lord nor did I know His Son. The Spirit of the Angel made me think of the things I had done. I never believed there was a hell until the Angel grabbed me and in the fire I fell. I only wish I would've been saved by this Jesus who arose from the grave. It's too late, I'm starting to feel the heat as my sins burn my flesh from my soul to my feet.

Birds

Birds fly through the air with their grace and charm. These little birds mean us no harm. They soar in flight like a feather in the wind. Sometimes a bird can be a friend. During the season, they play in the spring. the chirps, the sounds, and the songs they sing bring joy and laughter. With the things they do, they make one cheerful; when a bird comes to you.

The King

He was born in a manger. To some, just a stranger. Yet He was God in Man. He shed blood on a cross of love so we would understand. His heart was broken. Not a word was spoken as he hung and died. His memories, a token for all His children and for all mankind. His spirit ascended to Heaven from the cross that He wore. He was now in paradise. He reached the golden shore. Upon His return, He will reach us from the sky. To take us home with Him is the reason that He died. His death could never be in vain. He died for you and me. He's always been our Savior. That's why we call Him the King.

The Comforter

When life cuts deep and your heart is torn, remember God's love from the day you were born. For he has a plan, a plan for your life. If you give your all, he'll help you with strife. When your spirit is broken and you trudge all you can, remember they beat him and He was just a man. He'll bear your cross when life rips tears, and comfort your heart because He's always there. When your mind is gone and confusion is near, the grip of the Master will hold you dear. His shoulders are grand like the mountains we see. His love has the power to set the captive free. His spirit is strong and will flood through your life. When your days are long, He'll help you sleep at night. What would we do without our great King? If you kneel down before Him and continue to pray, love He will bring.

The Presence of God

I'm feeling the air with the presence of God and the love he has for me. The wind of the spirit blows through my heart, and today I know I'm free. Today I'm on a spiritual plane before I didn't see. Today I know God loves me, and today I'm just me.

911

The tower crumbled and lives were lost. Minds trembled from the holocaust. Hearts of anger filled the air. How could the bombers not even care? Rescuers came but it was too late, and at the hands of the bomber the innocents' fate. The memory will live on from the horror of 911 but God gathered his children and took them to heaven. The dust had cleared and a monument stood, and the families held on the best that they could. There wasn't much left after the dust, but a unified spirit for America they loved.

Hurt

The eyes of the innocent, overwhelmed with tears, and a mind diseased by fear. A rough patch along the way, pain and laughter clings to the breath of a hideous being. They have nothing to say. What goes around will come around and they will get their due. It's not for us to plan their wrath no matter what's done to you.

The End of the Ages

Time as we know it will someday pass away. But God will take his children and some of you will stay. It was written in a story and truth came to life. Jesus in his glory will come as a thief in the night.

The End of Me

When life shows up and I lose my mind, mountains of fear lie awake at the crest. It tears at my chest time after time. Moments of stillness lay awake in my reality, and a sudden burst of anger was my fatality. Powerful pain was within my heart and I couldn't let it go right from the start.

He Hears Your Cry

When your heart is burdened and you hurt inside, just remember God hears your cry. His blood poured out your sins that day and the days to come. He asked the cup to pass from him but he had you on his mind as he hung. Every drop of blood brought him closer to death, and he remained on the cross. Mary stood by, she heard her son cry. Then our father gave up the ghost.

The Cry of the Wind

The gale of the storm and the swell of the sea. The pain of life just won't let me be. I found a way to erase the past, but with the rise of the sea for air I gasped. Broken and thrown and tossed about, I cried to God, "Please, help me out." By the grief of the wake, my soul he did take. No longer do I cry to the wind. No longer do I shake.

Sober Freedom

Tranquility at its best, soaring in flight. Although I am all alone, I sleep so well at night. With all the calmness in the air, my wings please the sea. And when I'm finally safe at home, I'll be sober, loved, and free.

The Chosen One

If I died right now, I'd be in Heaven. I know this for a fact, my Spirit is clean. My sins are forgiven, there's nothing that I lack. I once had things, now they're gone. They've turned away from me. I didn't need them anyway. They just made me bleed. No wealth, no power, prestige is none, but I'm a child of the chosen one. Jesus Christ is his name He said this once to me, "Lose your life for my sake, in Heaven you will be."

Through the Fire

I was bound in cuffs, that wasn't enough. I'm doing time. It isn't rough. It's not that tough. I haven't lost my mind. I like my visits when they come. It's my heart's desire. There's no reason for me to run, I'll just walk right "through the fire." There's a plan, I know it's true. God holds the key. I know my future is in his hands; He knows what's best for me. It's not for me to decide whichever way I go. But I'm always on His mind through the trails of life I know.

Beneath the Willow

Tranquil as the sun for all the world to see. Alone, I'm free. Peaceful mountains all around, not a care, not the slightest sound. Apart from tragedy, strain, and distraught, the quietness of life and the stillness sought. A gentle breeze now and then from the willow, and I feel the wind.

This Heart

If you want material wealth, I have none to give. I offer you my only self for as long as we shall live. My heart was made by special hands, the crafters from above. For He gave his special plan, and we call it love. If you see this heart of mine, it's only flesh and blood. But if you look real deep inside, there you'll find my love. It's very strange and very shy, and oftentimes will hide. But when it sees a pretty smile, love is found inside. It's fragile; can be broken, can be ripped apart. When unkind words are spoken, you're messing with my heart. If it's cradled and it's loved, this heart is always there, and if you mean the love you say, this heart will always care.

What is a Friend

A friend is a treasure more precious than gold. They'll be by your side even when you get old. A friend will listen when you're in pain, and a friend will love you and never change. A friend will know when your heart is torn. A friend will care when your life is scorned. A friend won't judge you for the things you've done, but a friend will hold you when your tears began to run. A friend will bring happiness to your life, and a friend will be there through your strife. When you cry out and you feel you've reached the end, just lift up your eyes and look at your friend. A friend can touch you when no one can, because they know your life and truly understand. A friend will make you laugh because their laughter is a gift created by God for your spiritual lift. When you're down, can't think, can't go no more, a friend will quickly be at your door. A friend is an angel of a special kind given to you with your heart in mind.

Suicide

I know it hurts. It's in my mind. It's something I can't erase. If I had thought before this time, I would've sought the master's face. I think it's really too late now for me to change my mind. But my thoughts are racing anyhow, and I feel that now it's time. It's taking a lot to do this thing. It will be over in a while. My eyes are starting to rain with tears. I'm yearning for a smile. If God would only intervene, I could change my mind. If he would just erase this scene, just maybe I wouldn't die. If I could only feel his love and know that he is near, and I could only grip his hand he would hold me dear. I would consider stepping back, to try and rethink my plan. And if one could say, they love me now, I just might understand.

Loss of a Tranquil Mind

The Earth swallowed me up. The emotional grip and circumstances tore at my flesh; ripped off pieces clutched by fire of my burning soul. A treacherous climb to existence. Feeling of trouble, quoted by resistance. Looking for God and plea after plea. Sorrow of pain. Peace is coming. Acceptance is on its way but isn't here yet. A threat, a desire to feel again. The stage of the role, or honor to make things right. The blossom of the touch of the agreement toward saneness and tranquility. The flush of the decaying Spirit brought back to reality.

He Changed His Mind

From the moment of the flood, God changed his mind for he knew of the blood that his son would die. He placed his bow in the sky, and the earth wouldn't flood again. These were waters that he cried because of all man's sin. He found the one he could trust, and Noah was his name. But for all the sin and lust, the earth was not the same. Noah built an altar for his God above, and never did he falter because of all his love. He was perfect in God's sight. His heart was clean and pure, but when the raging waters came he knew he must endure. Noah stood strong through all of this trial and knew it would only last just for a while. All his faith he did keep, and the goodness that he sowed and all the treasures he did reap by the faithfulness he showed. If we could be like Noah just for a day, oh what treasures we would keep because of our faith. Sometimes we question just the reason why. If we could be like Noah, we wouldn't be afraid to die.

Safe in His Arms

God teaches us lessons all through our life. To help us understand the ways of the world and the foolish pride. We'll trust in our Lord and suffer no harm. For we know always we're safe in his arms.

Somewhere in the Clouds

I know that you hear me. You're somewhere in the clouds. I feel you're near me; your whisper I hear loud. You left me standing long ago, but today you're with the angels, this I truly know. What's it like in heaven today? Do you talk to Jesus and kneel down and pray? Do the angels sing a beautiful song? We miss your love now that you're gone. I'll need a hug when I see you again. I love you always and think of you now and then. I cry many tears, all that I can. With the years I hope you understand. It wasn't my time when you left this earth, but I keep you in mind. I've known you since birth. You will always have a place in my heart and I'm so sorry that we had to part. With your love, I'll think of you for now. Until one day, I'll meet you in the clouds.

Dialogue of Resentment

Crushed by despair, consumed by hate and emotional fire, life's too late. Battered and burned by another's grip. To find a way out for I lash from my lips, twisted and torn a robot design; to seek and destroy, to search and find. To seek and devour this horrid foe. To watch by the hour and never let go!

The Spiritual Wind

It rushes through my body, to this there is no end. The power deep inside is the power from a friend. It's mighty and it's strong. When my days are dead, it blows through my mind as I lie here in bed. Sometimes I cry and I think it's the end. But then it begins to rise, this spiritual wind. The wind will sustain me, as long as I care. For God is my temple. Yes He's always there. When life seems darkened, I begin to bend. I'll hold on to God and ride the Spiritual wind.

Dry Bones

Dead, buried deep in the earth. The enriched soil, of devour, mind racing thoughts, engulfed, by life. Spiritual nonexistence, limited faith, taken to the grave. No skin remains but disheartened luck. No change, broken dreams, and the need for rejuvenation but only valleys, of darkness until one sees the face of God.

When Mountains Fall

When mountains fall they crumble to the ground and break apart by the crush, by the sound. They fall until there's nothing left at all. Their cries call out from the pain. From the anger, from the stress, from the strain. Hardships and trials of life, undying rage with constant displays. Wrong or right to rip us and tear us and break us at the seams. The mountains fall and so does everything. The rocks separate one piece at a time; the broken foundation so heartless, so unkind. What happened to the mountain of love? The strength to the end. The mountain was a heart broken within.

I'm Locked in My World

I'm locked in my world all alone; safe at home. The sun is bright but my mind begins to roam. Although I sit and stare at the sky. If I had wings today I would fly. Away with the wind and carried so far, I would find myself an island; at night a star. White sand beaches with palm trees all around. If I could fly, my feet would never touch the ground.

A Crooked Mile

A crooked mile must be straight before I fall and it's too late. It's up to me to change the road for the crooked mile is getting old. I know the way to the right path, but the crooked mile is full of wrath.

In The Heart of Man

A man's heart plans his way, but the Lord directs his steps. He knows the path that he must take when his Savior is all that's left. But in his heart deep inside, the man feels nothing at all. He knows himself oh so well, but he's headed for a fall. A dangerous way he must go. He trudges by his will. He forgot that he was saved; in his heart he didn't feel.

Earthly Treasures

Diamonds, rubies, sapphires, and pearls are only a sinner's dream. They fill their pockets to the brim for Jesus they cannot see. They only think of more and more, the treasures on the earth. What about the gold, the frankincense, and myrrh? If one could satisfy the desire of their heart, put away the worldly life and find a new start. Where do riches lay? Where moth and dust corrupt? Or do you sometimes say "enough is never enough"?

The Price for Obedience

All through life ministered by change, we are slaves to sin. There comes a day, sometimes a night, we feel we've reached the end. With nowhere to hide, the pain inside is just too much to bear. But through the clouds, a nailscarred hand tells us God is there. When we accept the cross, we begin to live. Unless we're on bended knees, we can't receive the gift.

The Angel of Death

Last night I had a dream I descended to hell! I didn't believe the Bible, thought it was a fairytale. There was fire and brimstone, a place where evil lies. Dark angels carried me to my death as I bid this world goodbye. I screamed and I cried. Save me Lord from this terrible dream. I hear your voice but my eyes cannot see.

The Second Coming

As the spirit flows within me, I'm lifted up on high because I know that God's above as I look to the sky. A day will come when Christ will part and roll the clouds away. At this time I'm looking East, but for now I'll pray. He'll place his foot upon a hill and one upon the sea. With all His glory and His might, He will set us free. No one knows the time or day our King will arrive; and the sounds of trumpets the angels play, we'll be hearing from the sky. Will we be ready when He comes to take us far away? Or when we see him, will we run for the sin we've displayed? No matter where we try to hide, it will be too late. For our Master bled inside for this very day. So if we know we're full of sin and we must repent, God will be upon us all when our life is spent. Make sure that you are ready and that your heart is right, because we know that He will come like a thief in the night.

My Golden Glove

The power comes from my hand, and the keys are in my head. When the fire is lit my words come alive by the blaze of a romantic torch. I continue to write words of love held together like pieces of fine thread. My inspiration comes from above, and the spirit from heaven reaches my golden glove.

The Child that I am

In this holy place, there is refuge for my soul. I come to the father for I have nowhere else to go. He cradles me and rocks me like a baby in His arms. I feel his love around me when He wraps me with His scars. Angels rejoice as I sit on daddy's lap, and he holds me to his chest, it's time for a little nap. I grip his garment and I can't let go. Only the master's love is all that I know. He eases my sorrow and heals all my pain. My father, my Lord knows my name. For all of my hardships I couldn't understand, but my belief in Jesus makes me the child that I am.

The Turtle

Shielded from the enemies outside of myself, I cling to my innards to deal with nothing else. Occasional sunlight is all I require, and a breath of fresh air is my only heart's desire. A dominant one may want to crush my shell, but my instincts tell me "get inside" where I dwell. Slowly with caution, I move throughout my day. I'm a little turtle and I know where I'm safe.

When Tears Begin to Fall (He Hears Your Cry)

When your tears begin to fall on a cold rainy night, it's not your battle, it's God's fight. You try to live for Jesus the best way you can, but somehow you're broken and live in a lonely land. It's you against the world and this is how it seems, but our sovereign Lord sees everything. Paul said "stand and continue to stand, and glorify the Lord; reach for his hand."

Satan's Enemy

Who has the last word when the devil has you down? God's wrath will come when you're tossed all around. Just keep the faith and trust in Christ. He sees your hurt all through the night. He loves you more than you'll ever know. His mighty power he will always show. The devil is a loudmouth, our savior sees his rage. But he also knows he has numbered his days. Be not afraid when Satan comes at you. Your spirit will bind him, and Jesus will sustain you.

On a Lonely Road

It's not easy to be a Christian when rejected by the world, but it's worth the precious crown spoken in the word. Dust off your feet when you are turned away, and lift up your hands when you kneel down to pray. Haters scoffed at Jesus before you came along; persecuting Christians is just the same ole' song. Be not discouraged. You'll have a crown of gold. But for now you're on a lonely road.

The Throne of Grace

When, I am discouraged, I seek, the master' s face. I remember, the cross, bow my head, and pray. When, my heart, is broken, and it seems, there, is no way, I, think of the blood of Jesus, and the throne, of grace. When, my mind, is confused, and something, happens today, I'll fall, on my knees, and see, the look, on his face. I, remember the thorns, placed upon his head, I know, it should've, been me instead. I can't imagine, that dreadful place, but I know, it's over, he's, on the throne, of grace.

The Day He Set Me Free

I walked, through a garden, on a cold, damp mourn, and my eyes, had begun, to rain. The mist, of my tears, fell to the ground, my heart, was grieved, with pain. The garden, seemed, forever, like there, was just no end. I, forced myself, through the weather, and laid in my sin.

An angel came, before me, as I stayed fast asleep. My father, in heaven, adored me, but his eyes, began, to weep. He said, "to the angels, bring my child, "to me, and he washed me, with his blood, the day, he set me free.

A Divine Purpose

Don't ask me why, I'm still here, but god, has a plan, so why, should, I fear, or shed a tear? Peace, and joy, and hope, for the coming. Waves, of splendor, shall encompass, my being.

God, knows, the reason; although, I don't see him. My flesh and form, still has life, a divine purpose, will come, in his time.

The Eastern Corner of My Window

The Eastern corner of my window is oh so very small. I think of a place called heaven, or I think of nothing at all. To God, I am a gentleman by the peace he's given me. He sees my heart, it's full of joy and he lets me just be me. When he looks down at me he hopes I'll pray again, and hopes one day I'll talk with him now and then.

I'm Just Me

I'm feeling the air with the presence of God and the love he has for me. The wind of his spirit blows through my heart, and today I know I'm free. Today I'm on a spiritual plane but before I didn't see. I know God loves me, and I love that I'm just me.

Tired Eyes

My eyes are weary as I look into the mirror. My reflection was foggy but is now somewhat clearer. I see the life that I have succumbed to. My eyes see many things without a compass. My future lies in wait.

Shattered Heart

A day will bring pain in life, we just don't understand. It makes us think of who we are and God holds our hand. The choices we made are over now, but we made it through. God always gave us strength somehow, and he showed us what to do. We looked inside to see the wrong and had to keep our mind. For us we had to be strong, then a new treasure we would find. Our mind was bent and burdened, it had torn us all apart with all the many pains from the crush of a broken heart. We contemplated other things needed for our growth, but instead our heart had suffered from things we didn't know.

He Knows You're Alone

If God could reach inside your heart, what would He find there? A smile, a frown, a mile of parts no one really cares? He gives us love and gives us life, but our world is bitter and tom because of all the selfish ways we've had since we were born. When your spirit is crowded with so much pain, you feel you have no home. But if you'll only just remain, you'll never be alone. He said he'd stick by your side no matter what you'd face. For His Son gave His life with His solemn grace. So please don't fear when you are hurt and your mind begins to roam, our God above hears your cry, and now you're not alone.

If I Could Wave a Magic Wand

What can I do to stop your pain when you begin to cry? I try to see inside your heart, the rain within your eyes. A burden as strong as this, I know it gets you down. Can I touch you with a kiss and please don't make a sound? I'm not a wizard nor a magical being, and I'm not a fairytale. But if I had a wish for you, I would rid you from this spell.

Possible Fate

When I think of you there's beauty in your eyes. Sparkles of sunshine like the blue in the sky. The thought of you grabs my heart and just won't let go. My body yearns and cries for your affection. My mind races and my spirit pours out the love. I feel for you. Your words touch me softly, and your grace and charm molds your inner beauty. A fire burns within my soul when I see you smile. Your gentleness and emotional touch grasp every part of my inner being. The likeness of your spirit and the common bond we share make me think possible fate is in the air.

Rose Petals

This token that I give to you is from a lonely heart. I knew the things I put you through from the very start. I wish I would have tried again, I could've been much more of a friend. Honey, please forgive me for what I've said and done. I'll try to make it up to you if you will not run. The mistakes I've made have cursed your heart. I can't undo the past. If I'm just given one more chance, I know our love will last. How can I prove to you I'll change day by day? I know I truly have broken your heart, but I promise you I'll stay. With this rose I give to you, please hold it in your hand. Because you know when I'm with you, I'm your only man. I know your heart was shattered, and I know it aches and mourns. Please, take this token with my love, and for you I will adorn.

Can You Still Believe in Me?

Last night we had a fight. It wasn't right and my mind was tight. You blamed me and I blamed you, but you know it wasn't true. Words were thrown back and forth, then silence touched the ground. You were hurt and I was sore. At once there was no sound. I tried my best to make it right but you wouldn't talk to me. You sat and stared as we took a ride, so I just let you be. I wish I knew what I did to break your little heart. Please, forgive me. My mind was spun. I know we needed a new start. My stomach turned because of this pain, and it made you very sad. Tell me things that I can do to turn this thing around. If we can talk and see it through, please just make a sound. My mind will speak a dummy's tone and say the wrong things. I forget to engage my brain, can you still believe in me?

Still Searching

Many times I thought I had love but it all turned to stone. Always a glitch in my quest for love, I found myself alone. No matter just how hard I tried, it just wasn't there. At times I gave up and said, "I really don't care. I'm a good person as you can see, what is it that is wrong with me?" You say I'm not your cup of tea. "You, go away. You say you want to be free." I try and try again hoping you'll be my friend. I'll be searching to the end.

Until We Meet Again

I think of you when you're away. I'm sad you're not here today. The thought of you is always on my mind as I look back on our good times. If it's written in the stars, I know, honey, you won't go far. If I could hold you one more time, I know I would be just fine. It won't happen today, so I pray we'll be together some day. I don't have the power to control or stop what has been placed by the will of God. I only know just how I feel, and my love for you is very real. For a place in time, we are only friends. You're engraved in my mind until we meet again. I sit, drink some coffee, and try to relax, and I ponder and wonder if you will ever be back. My mind sees your beauty and it's so clear to me. A special painted picture of your memory. I yearn to be held by you, a love that shines through and through. You're an angel with a grin, an angel with a smile. In my mind, you will always be. I'll hold steadfast to your memory. I still think of you now and then, and I'll just wait until we meet again.

Our Magical Love

Silence in the Spring, a soft kiss from the air. Within, warm feelings of honesty between us. Fantasies and realities of romance we treasure. Dreams solidify and encompass our being together as one. Sprinkles of love slowly rain down. Two hearts of tender mercy joins our souls. In the end, we love until were old.

The Battleground

I know the mines were placed in the land and the commander in chief had to make a stand. The blood of the soldiers would come again and again. A ruler of power, a leader of hell was never a friend. Saddam was a killer of the Iraqi people; the war was all in vain. A man who didn't care about women and children could've only been insane. One day he'll answer for the blood that was shed, and his day of judgment is coming ahead. Osama Bin Laden, such a murderer you are, and I say God help you, you won't go far. The will of our God is much stronger than you. You can hide all you want but you're sealing your doom. A machine of disaster you have become. Women feared for their life and all they could do was run. A war is a battle one never wins, for peace and harmony dies in the end. Our soldiers cry tears for the families they left. You'll be sealed in a tomb because of your theft. A God of this earth you thought you would be, but you sealed your fate and you will never go free. On the day of judgment, I'll feel for you. You will stand before God and shake in your boots. We are God's children we've known, this from birth, and do you think you could ever rule the earth? When it rains day after day, God cries for our soldiers but he knows they must stay. An armchair warrior you have become; a king of death by the power of your gun. Your mind must be chained by the horror you caused. Your brain played tricks on you, and for all the destruction, the holocaust, there's no hope for you.

Old Centralia Road

On this old road, I walked to school mile after mile in the snow. With books in hand I trudged the way, I knew which way to go. Each morning I'd wake up and Granny would sing and play her guitar just for me. "A sunbeam, a sunbeam. Jesus wants me for a sunbeam." I remember words like music from her lips, and I would sit and listen on Granny's hip. She hugged me and loved me each and every morn, but one day she went to Heaven to be with the Lord.

Eternity

When Jesus comes, where will you be? Will your heart be troubled when the Son you'll see? With the Angels of Glory and His power and might, He will come to take us "like a thief in the night." In the clouds of Heaven I want to see him someday, but until that time comes let's continue to pray. The sinner doesn't know Him, but they will wish they did. And if they receive Him, forever they will live.

The Last Supper

He broke bread with his children. He knew this would be the last time. For he knew a moment would follow. Yes He knew He would die. Jesus went to the gallows to be hung for our sins. The Savior went to die but we know He's coming again. Jesus went to the gallows knowing what would happen to Him. He shed His life blood there for all of our sins. The road was heavy with burden as he carried the cross to the hill, and although we were pardoned for crimes we did with our will.

The Eye of the Savior

On a cross He died, He gave His life for me. He bled from His side as he hung on the tree. His body was broken, His heart still had love. Jesus is His name, He was sent from above. The shame and torment no other could bear. Scoffers laughed but his mother really cared. She cried in pain as she watched her son die, but as she gazed at him she saw the look in his eyes.

Lonely Heart

A silent conclusion to a past gone wrong, and waves of depression the only song. No tears of joy throughout each day. Conscious thoughts, mistakes I've made, and things I hold onto can never be saved. The want to live a victorious life to rid the pain from all the strife. A lonely heart is sad but true. It won't last forever just because of you.

The First Day

My mind is drifting so far as I gaze at the moon and the stars. You know what I feel. You know that it's real, and I know of your hidden scars. You must have your time to straighten out your mind for your journey has been deadened, but you are alive. And you're clean this time for your secrets no longer are hidden. You have your place and I must believe who you truly are. Because when I look at the sky, I see your face. You are the brightest star. The heart will never change, recovery's often strange. But when you fly your spirit will cry, and you'll never be the same.

The Unbreakable Truth

The word of God is salvation to the soul, and it's given to all who just can't let go. The sword and spirit this word portrays is the path to righteousness through all our days. When we have placed his word on our heart, we find the unbreakable truth. We should've known this from the very start.

When Grown Men Cry

As a tear falls from his eyes, a little boy breaks inside. Silent pain that no one can see when his heart begins to grieve. Tall in stature, he's a man. But engulfed by hurt, you wouldn't understand.

In My Dreams

A place in time, a special scene, and the thought of love, only a memory. I had my chance to make it right but it wasn't meant to be. This love is lost and won't return but only in my dreams. I'll shed a tear from time to time, and with it comes pain. No matter how much I try and try, I'll never see her again. The hurt belongs within my heart until I set it free. Still the truth remains in my mind, but only in my dreams.

A Field of Loneliness

I walked through this field with life all around, and no one at the time was there. No feeling in the midst, no sight or sound, and nobody seemed to care. I held my head to the ground then I began to cry. My head was spinning all around, as I reached for this child inside. Although my thoughts had been misplaced, I stood there for a while. My past had finally been erased as I hugged this little child.

Parental Warriors

What gave you the right to possess a sword, and by your forked tongue you lashed out with words? Who made you have demon eyes of blood? You don't live with the scars, your children do. Were we so bad we had to have your grief burned into our brains? When you laid down the law, even God backed away. You created the steel heads we possess, the rebellion, and the hate. Every word you said crushed our bones with your breath, and when you stopped breathing fire, you said you loved us. Were you a liar?

$\mathcal{L}$oneliness

Loneliness is a plague which burns through my very loin. It burns like fire within my eyes. My tears are red with blood-drenched sorrow from my past. My heart cries with grief because no one is here. I yearn for that special someone to brighten my life and quench my thirst. Inside I die one more hour. I'm distraught by this power. I'm intrigued by one clear thought that maybe I'm just alone tonight.

The night Becomes

I fell to the night fast asleep. I stepped into the river of life. I couldn't feel my feet touch the ground, but my body was free in flight. Surrounded by bubbles I had begun to drown. The light was above and a few feet away, I couldn't make a sound. Silently I prayed. "Lord, save me from this river of fright. Please, wake me up from this horrible night."

Push

Strained by desire for others to destroy. A motive to conquer, to ruin a good ploy. Deceivers and doubters to strip you from success, and because of their insecurities they never let you rest. Bludgeoned, from the dust of evil plans and crushed by remembrance from the lies within their hands. Someone you once knew, to honor, hold and love, but drained you from your life by their mouth. They took your blood.

Under The Stairs

I put together words as I write beneath the stairs. Another day in prison where life isn't fair. I know it's worse for others, the time they have to spend. But my heart cries for moments I had outside the fence. Alone in a fortress, but people fill the walls. And locked in time with little hope at all. I know the day will come when my mind has been released. It's just a day, for now under the stairs, that I'm free.

The Inmate Way

One day in the rain I found myself in chains. It was over in a flash.
Behind steel doors, I was on the floor thinking of where I was at.
There were knots inside me, no place to hide me from the stories I
heard before. The world I knew was gone. I found myself alone, like
a ship lost in a storm. I learned how to talk. I learned how to walk.
It was the inmate way. This would be my home, the streets were all
gone. I didn't have a choice but to stay. I'm in here now, for a min-
ute somehow, and I sit and watch the cars. I think of the choices I
could've made, as God heals my scars.

The Rock

A cornerstone of love, God is my rock. A flowing river from above a spiritual fountain. A mountain of peace that will heal a broken heart. The undying care of one who is lost and from His palms, gave His son to pay the cost. A mind twisted and tortured within. My Savior has come to try to be my friend. A painful past, memories of discord, erased by His grace and changed by His word.

A Broken Heart That's Crying

Don't hold back even one tear when your heart cries with pain. It's only part of the sum of life. It's just a little rain. Yes, it's true your mind is torn and thoughts are everywhere. But maybe it's time to see inside a heart that really cares. A moment spent with you could change you all around. Please, don't let the thunder roll and crash you to the ground. God knows where you are right now, it was written in His book. And now your heart is telling you, there is peace where you look. When your eyes behold the past, just kneel down and pray, because we know it doesn't last but just a minute and only for a day.

The Transition of Change

Before the dark gloom I once possessed is now a healing for others. Once my heart was very scorned, but now I love my brothers. My life is changing through a gradual twist that only I truly know, and the death of life within my mind is my resurrected soul. Through all the pain, the guilt and shame, I found my place in life. To help and love as time remains, today this is my plight. Though often torn and ripped apart, I find solace in my God. For He knows, without a doubt, the many steps I've trod. Through His love and mercy, and the greatness that He shows, I'll cling to Him with all I have because He truly knows. He knew me then and knows me now, and the future which is held. By the palm of His hand, some way somehow, He's always been my shield. My protector and provider, God has always been. And through this transition of change, He's always been my friend.

I Wish It was Just a Dream

I can't believe that I'm in here, apart from all the world. I didn't plan my life this way with all this turmoil. I should've listened to my peers when they talked to me. They were wise in what they said. It's something I just couldn't see. Evil lurks in different ways, it traps and brings you down. You don't know until you're snared, then you're chained and bound. There's a map. It's the book to guide and direct our path. If we don't take the time to look, we'll reap a deadly wrath. It's too late, the time has come, and its only jail for me. I never thought that I would be here, I wish it was just a dream.

A Sinner's Prayer

Sweet Jesus, sweet Jesus, come unto me, please! Give me your inner peace. I know you will if I call on you for you will show me just what to do. When my head is spent and done, I know you'll help me so I won't run. I know in the valleys you're always there because I know in my heart you really do care. I know God if I stay clean you will always be there for me. If my gift is rushed before it's time, I know I'll lose it before it's mine. With all the lessons I must learn while I'm in the valley, to you I'll turn. I believe you knew me then and you know me now, with all my troubles and my sin you loved me anyhow.

Unknown Fear

My mind says, "Don't cry, it's only thunder." But my fear makes me wonder what will come next. Will it strike North, South, East, or West? My faith must be surmounted with prayer. I must believe I'll be alright; that God's somewhere. I try to not think of this pain but it's in my brain. The tunnel is dark with only a little light, but as long as I breathe I'll fight. Twenty-four is all I have so I can't be sad. This happened for a reason, there's a meaning in the clouds. I must grab a prayer from my heart and give it to God right now. Brief moments I'll break inside, but God sustains me. This power of this evil is more than I can bear. And this unknown fear, it rips and it tears.

A Walk Through Pain

I walked away from the words of my mother, the instruction of my father which would have sustained me. I forgot the sea; that I could be forgiven. Rebellion is all I knew; I carry the symbol on my arm. There is a throne in Heaven and my sovereign Lord sits upon it, seated at God's right hand.

The Ice Cap

I force my pick into the snow. As I climb to the top of the mountain, I won't let go. One slip from life will cause me to fall. I must continue my quest for survival, but the mountain is so tall. A rope will fuse me to the side of this mountain as onward I go in this journey in the snow, the rain, and the cold. When I reach the top I can rest my weary head. I'll pitch me a tent, and relax, and go to bed.

My Lonely Existence

All around me, people cheer for the love they have of someone near. It seems as though their life's complete, but I yearn for a love, for someone to meet. Before in my past, at times I had a love I thought would last.

Tears

With every drop I sit and wonder about my future. My brain is so burned by my bridges. Life has become rigid. There isn't enough water in the ocean to explain how I feel. Life is real. I hope and pray life will improve before I lose myself.

The Burden

He carried our burden to the cross. He knew me and you. He died for the lonely and the lost, and bled through and through. He had us in mind when came the time to give up the ghost. For in the land Jesus took a stand, for He loved us the most.

Peace

If I had peace, where would I be? My mind would be set free! From the snares of life through all the strife, I could just be me. The love of God is all we have and it's all we need. He'll reach around with arms of love and comfort us with peace.

Life Ever So Changing

A journey in time, the past we have found. Mistakes we've all made sometimes brought us down. We dwelled in the hate, discord, and the wrath. We live without hope from our self-driven path. Love is not found, and light-years away. We continue to struggle day after day. No solace is placed in our heart or our mind. Until we start to pray, our soul we'll never find.

Flight to Freedom

I must accept today for all that God has made. He gave us life to love from His heart above. The will we have is strong and controls our every move. We'll keep this for too long, and we begin to lose. So put your faith in Him and let Him guide your path. And if you cleave to God, the life you have will last. Our mind will play tricks and so many games, to the point we use and were never the same. If we have our trust, and recovery is the key, the prisoner in our head will someday be set free. Our new life is strange; it's quirky and it's weird. When our moods change, it's God we'll hold dear. We know this life is new and the choice we have is ours, and when we're asked how we got there, it was written in the stars. Some will fall and some will fail, and the winner will prevail. But the love we share will keep us in His care, for the flight to freedom we'll sail.

A Mothers Love

How do you compare a Mother's precious love, only a given treasure from our God above? She'll hold you and keep you in her loving care, and when you get older she is always there. She'll teach you ways that are only good. If you do what she says, you'll do what you should. Oftentimes we go astray but she'll pray for us that very day. Her instincts will tell her she has a child in trouble. She'll drop what she's doing and be there on the double. When she sees your tears and your pain, she never changes, she's always the same. She'll cradle you in her arms for life, and uphold you through all your strife. A mother is a special gift, and when your down she'll give you a lift. She's stern and strong when she has to be, but a mother's precious love was made for you and me.

The Gift That He Gave

On the day before Christmas, His spirit came to me. What is the meaning of the presents by the tree? Only a symbol of our savior's birth. The gifts from the wise men of gold, frankincense, and myrrh. It's all about the cross where Jesus bled and died. To save the lost sinners, He was crucified. It's not about Santa Claus, or gifts for you and me. It's all about our savior, how he set us free. Remember the star that led the wise men that day. It's all about the garden where he kneeled down to pray. It's all about the time where Jesus bled and died. He had us on his mind when he was crucified.

Is It Really All About Me and You?

When I feel it's convenient, can I really find the time? To serve the master of heaven, are His treasures really mine? Do I always read my Bible and talk of Jesus too? Or do I rest on my laurels and forget all about you? Do I study the Sunday lesson; help those in dire need? Do I spend all my money because of my greed? Am I a good Samaritan or just a passerby? Have I given my life to Jesus? If not, He knows why! Do I help the sick and afflicted? Do I feed hungry mouths? Am I really a Christian? I'll search my spirit right now! Have I done all I can to carry his message, too? Ask yourself this simple thing, is it really all about me and you?

Broken

Grief struck his heart as he cried tears of blood, but what was to come could've only been his love. He was bound by the soldiers and placed before the king. Jesus stood in silence and didn't say a thing. As he stood in fear, the scoffers had their day. And God saw his Son, what a dreadful place. Spikes splintered his bones and blood gushed from his side, and his mother could do nothing but cry.

Words

What are words to you and me, only gifts that we can see. The power of words reach to others. The power of words blow our cover. Words can hurt, and words can heal. Words can search, and words can reveal. Words are thoughts, and thoughts are words. Words are silent, and sometimes heard. Words can change, words can hide. Words are complete, and words are simplified.

Codependent Me

This hole is empty. I can't fill it. I use others to satisfy my needs this codependency disease. I'm not real. This drug is a pill. I play with their heart until I rip it apart but I can't reveal it. Still it's locked in my brain. It's driving me insane. I pray that's my gain on what I can't have until I drive them all away, and that's very sad where I can't even feel it. It's hard to live by yourself when you're accustomed to this codependent hell! I know the key that will set me free: it's honesty. I get lonely and try to cope. I'm okay without this dope. I think it's alright, these things I do, because I'm sucked up in this vacuum tube. My brain is fickle, confused and scared and, when the drug is gone I feel so impaired. I know it's a problem of magnitude and cause. If I want to get healthy, I'll take time and pause. I'm powerless over the demon's grip. I can't control it, so I continue to slip. I don't eat it. I don't smoke it. It's not that kind of drug. It engulfs me and entangles me as soon as I am hugged.

A Mother's Day

A Mother's Day is a special day; a treasure of its own. A mother's love is a special love now that we are grown. A mother's heart is a special heart and known since we were birthed which helped us through our trying times while living on God's Earth. A mother's soul is a special soul; the instincts are within. Mother's care is always there when we just need a friend. A mother's mind is a special mind when they can see our hurt. A mother's arms cradle us with love when we hunger and we thirst. A mother's spirit will cry for God when we are down and have fallen to the ground. A mother's peace will calm our lives and whisper with a sound. A mother's laughter is full of joy and given with a smile. When far away she knows that day, and prays for us awhile.

The Master of the Clouds

Today my Father is above. I feel safe in His love. I know I'm His child. I know I was once wild but I have the spirit of a dove. This rushing mighty wind inside fills my every being. I know He's there. I know He cares even though I don't see Him. Engulfed by Angels, I'm protected every day and always will be as long as I pray.

His Undying Love

To gather all jewels and wealth that we see, we credit ourselves by spiritual disease. We think it's ours and never satisfied, but with His undying love He was crucified. We spend our days flowing with the wind, often taking for granted our Spirit within. God doesn't exist in some of our minds, but when we are hurt it's time we try to find. Caught up in a world of earthly deceit, let's remember the cross. He died for you and me.

Crippled by a Plague

Life is vague, no end in sight; the futures is in the air, I can't sleep at night, and I really don't care. A pillar of strength, and a pillar is sought. I'm bound and hurt, by all my thoughts. My broken mind is alone this time, donned by an attitude of injustice. Meaningful bliss, doesn't exist; peace and serenity has escaped my heart. Piercing arrows have shattered pieces of my life. Swords of anger and revenge and distance away again and again, without a friend.

Crippled, by a plague, I feel my sin; it only lies within.

My Loving Father

Good morning! Lord, how are you? From your throne of Grace, you'll see me through! You know my heart. Why should I fret with all my frailties yet you still love me? From this winding road you've given me peace and my love for you shall never cease! Oh! What a pleasure to know you're above. Oh! What a treasure. It's your undying love. Although I stumble and I fall, your grace will sustain me through it all!

The Abandoned Child

I woke up one day and no one would play. I sat and stared at them. No one would say, "Please! Come here and play. You can be my friend." I felt so lost and my mind was tossed. I didn't understand, I wanted love like them. I sat for a while and tried to smile, but I had no peace within.

The Rapture

Last night I went to heaven and I left the earth behind. First, I saw the master with his arms open wide. His garment was white; it was white as snow. I saw the holes in his hands from the blood that flowed. The angels bowed before him as they took their places at his feet. They smiled with their eyes and began to spread their wings. The spirit of God flooded my soul. Jesus and I walked on streets of purest gold. Not once could I ever take my eyes off of him, and now I was in heaven walking with my friend. I saw a man in the distance with a staff in his hand. All the disciples came one at a time, then they stood before Jesus and they gazed in my eyes. At the end of the road was the mighty throne of grace. I saw God the Father and the glow on his face. God sit calmly with power and might. I was summoned to the throne, and oh what a sight! He opened a book and my name was laid in gold, and God began to talk as he sat on his throne. "You've proven to be like Jesus, my son. Your earthly battle is over and the victory is now won."

It's Bigger Than I

This problem I have is deep and wide; it travels many miles throughout my mind. I ponder and wonder because of my fear, but I believe in you Lord and I'll hold you near. The magnitude of thought bleeds my brain, but I know Lord you'll help me deal with the pain. The end seems so far away, but Lord you're holding me today. I know if I put my trust in you, Lord, I know you'll see me through! I know that Faith I truly must have, and Lord you'll wipe my tears when I'm sad. At times I seem I'll just fall apart, but Lord I know you'll help me because you're in my heart.

When Jesus Died to Live

Easter is the time of year for all to celebrate. God raised Jesus from the grave. We remember the day. Baskets filled with candy, eggs hidden behind a tree. Children with their laughter, running wild and free. Happy times for every child when they receive their gift But what about the true delight when Jesus died to live?

The Mysteries of God

I wish I knew the mind of God but this is not my call. For the love that He gives is unconditional for the great and small. He's the Master, I am his servant. He knows the steps I've trod even if I was as big as a mountain. I'd never know the mysteries of God. He sits quietly, and conscientiously watches our every move. He knows all there is to know about us, and He loves us, too. We try to love as He does, but we're only human. He'll give his heart when we won't for our life which was given. He always hurts when we fall and cries for our safety. His heart will always break when we've denied Him lately. For this God that we serve is so gentle in spirit. He's the Counselor and the Prince of Peace so we must not fear Him. His promises will reach across our hearts and He will hold us there. For He's our loving Father above and He really cares. Have peace within yourself this very day for God knows you well. And you'll see Him someday for if you fall so short of Him after the steps you've trod, just be sure you'll know of Him, but never the knowledge of **God**!

About the Author

To tell you what inspired me to write the "The Mirror In The Brook", I have to begin, by first telling you, how it all begun. In 1988 I was rushed to the hospital by ambulance, I was suicidal. A Dr. by the name of Joseph Fontaine diagnosed me with " Borderline Personality Disorder " To this day, I've been in counseling (28 yrs.) People with this mental illness, have striking artistic abilities. I wrote, the mirror in the brook, at the lowest point in my life. I've been writing, for 16 yrs. One night in my guard shack (I worked security), I was thinking about a little boy looking into the water by a brook and he was wondering and searching for God, and he found his son Jesus.

CPSIA information can be obtained
at www.ICGtesting.com
Printed in the USA
BVHW071742210119
538283BV00004B/263/P